# U Have

*A Diary of Praise*

# Aretha Johnson

ISBN 979-8-88832-050-1 (paperback)
ISBN 979-8-88832-051-8 (digital)



Christian Faith Publishing
832 Park Avenue
Meadville, PA 16335
www.christianfaithpublishing.com

Printed in the United States of America

# CONTENTS

*Whatever you do, work at it with all
your heart, as working for the Lord.*

—Colossians 3:23 (NIV)

Most people that really know me know that I consider myself to be God's favored child. I'm His friend, and He loves me. I'm not being arrogant nor uppity. I'm just saying what His Word tells me. It's right there in the book of Proverbs 8:35 (NASB), which states, "*For whoever finds me, finds life and obtains favor from the Lord.*" I believe it and that settles it. Thus being favored, the idea of me keeping a diary of what He is doing during the various seasons of my life came to me approximately 3½ years ago, and I decided to be obedient and go for it. I've chosen some of the diary to share. Never did I think I would be at a point to consider getting it published. It's for me to catalogue my thoughts and life. After I've gone through this, maybe to get it at the published process, I'll read it again and probably shout my way through most of it. The subtitle, *A Diary of Praise*, is exactly what this is.

I hear a lot of people use the phrase "you just don't know my situation." I agree. None of us really knows what the other person is going through in their lives. True, we are all going through something at any given time. No one knows your story like you know your story. I have learned that whatever time you look at and think of anyone that they must really have their life together, start praying because they probably don't. For every person who ever said that to me—you have no idea. This is my praise diary of my journey.

This diary is for anyone else out there who's going through their life's storms and wondering, "Is there *anyone* else going through this same stuff? Am I the only one dealing with these issues?" The answer is adamantly *no*. You are not alone. While reading my diary, you may find something in here that you can relate to; you may not. I'm not saying you should praise your way through on your journey; however, I do highly recommend it.

I AM IN AWE!! I just finished your book, and I am a mess of emotions! Your writing is interesting. I couldn't stop reading; inspiring.

Aretha, did an awesome job in sharing your journey to becoming a wife, mother, and woman of God!

I hope that I and other readers will use the inspiration you've shared to keep our eyes on God and live the life He has for us, in its entirety.

Jeanne Vernon
"Life is Beautiful"

It's funny how God works.

I have to say that your book has truly blessed me. I laughed and cried!

Thank you for being obedient and sharing your diary with the world. It will truly bless many more.

Cherell Evans Latimer
Founder, A.C.E. Legaci Foundation
Author, Mentor

# ACKNOWLEDGEMENT

Special thanks to the following people who have blessed my life's journey:

- Absolutely, hands down, no doubt about it, the best husband a gal could dream of—Evan. Looking forward to what's next in our lives.
- The woman who taught me to be strong, serve God with all I have and how to show love to others and to never give up—Mrs. Dorothy Wells Smith-Jenkins.
- The man who was the example of what qualities to look for in a man for my own life—Mr. Willie Jack Jenkins. He's also the one who taught me my first bad word, Crapdabbit! LOL
- Our two wonderful sons. You both have made my life fun, funny, interesting, scary, and most definitely blessed. You both have improved/changed my prayer life. Keep on doing what you do and watch God continue to show up and show out in your lives. You have no idea!
- My family—simply stated—*I love you* all. You have no idea.
- God, thank You! *"I will bless the Lord at all times. His praise will continually be in my mouth"* (Psalm 34:1).

# CHAPTER 1

# The '80s, Inherited Blessings

As I sit here pondering life and rolodexing the chronicles of my life, I am astounded that the years have flown by. I am now eligible for the AARP card. Wow—when did this happen? I actually have the thought that I must have blacked out and awoken twenty years later. Surely, I was not having that much fun while living through the years of my twenties, thirties, and forties that fast! Apparently so.

Can I look back and say I had a blast of a great time? Yes, I can. Can I think back and wonder if it was all worth where it got me to today? Absolutely. Is there anything I would change? Nope. Changing it is not possible, and if it was, that would be scary. These thoughts bring me to what I was reading earlier today. Today's motivation has the phrase "start right where you are." That's what I'm doing. Right now. Today. This minute. Thus this book. I'm releasing some of my life's diary and telling my story while wondering what will come of this. Something? Nothing? Doesn't matter. I asked God about it, and this is where He led me. It is true. It is scary, and it is funny to me to think that this is my life. Definitely interesting.

Beginning in summer 1983, I was nineteen, naive, unwed, pregnant, and confident. Wow. Five scary words to describe me. Thankfully, I didn't listen to the naysayers and oh so "helpful" friends who said not to get married. I was told, "Girl, go get yourself on welfare and put his behind on child support!" None of that made sense to me. Particularly since the ones giving such advice did not know my baby's daddy and obviously didn't really know me. Did they not understand how I and my siblings were raised? Nope. My mama did not raise me with that mind-set. She too was confident, strong, and strongly believed in God, believing she could do all things through Him!

My mama was on crutches much of my life and confined to a wheelchair in her fiftyish and later years. Her attitude and demeanor were of such confidence that when I got in trouble in my childhood years, I actually thought she could and would let go of those crutches and run to catch me and I would get a good old-fashioned whooping for whatever I had done. In our house, you could find the neighborhood snack store or the kids' weekly Bible study, depending on what day it was. All effectively and productively ran by my mama from her wheelchair. That is the kind of confidence she instilled in me. In my early adulthood, I remember at one point thinking that she would actually get up and out of her wheelchair and grab me. That's the kind of confidence she instilled in me. Don't let my circumstances dictate me. I dictate my life with God as my head leader. That I should take everything to Him, and He will fix it. Depend on God, not man. So I'm nineteen and pretty dang confident...about everything.

I had that confident feeling about my baby's daddy. I recognized that he was different. I just had that deep-down instinctual gut feeling that he wouldn't fall into the category of a deadbeat dad. He wasn't going to be like the stereotypical deadbeat dad—Shanaynay's baby daddy. You know, the one who lived across town, ran around on her, and had two more kids on the other side of town by two other girls! Nope, my baby's daddy said we were getting married when he found out I was pregnant. I was the holdout. He didn't ask me. He told me several times. Special thanks to his parents for being the pioneers they were and smart enough to leave a heritage behind.

My baby's daddy had his own house and land. My baby's daddy worked two jobs. My baby's daddy was raised as a fine young Southern bred man with manners. My baby's daddy had big ideas, and we were going places and planned to do big things. My baby's daddy was named Evan. Evan knew how to shoot a shotgun dead bull's-eye straight.

I found out that little but very important tidbit after we got married. One beautiful summer day, we arrived home and pulled up in the driveway. I looked out across the yard. What do you know, a *long* black snake (about six feet long, seriously) was stretched out across in the yard, sunning itself! Well, you know what happened next. I freaked out. Hollering, crying…yep, the whole nine yards. No matter what, I was not getting out of that car! Now, right here, I'll stop and apologize to all of you creature lovers out there. *I do not like snakes.* Never have and never will.

Evan to the rescue. He put the car in park, ran in the house, grabbed the shotgun, and came running back out. He took aim and proceeded to scare out what air I had left in my lungs. Yes, he scared me speechless. Of course, my ears were not working at that point as I really wasn't expecting the shotgun to be so loud! I'd never heard one being shot before this. At that point, loss of speech and hearing were the last things on my mind. I just needed my eyes to see and know that the snake was no longer among the land of the living. Last I checked, from very far away that snake's head was blown to smithereens. I love you, Lord, but could you please get rid of these creatures!

Neither I nor Evan planned for life. We were happy doing what most young couples do. Living life in a bubble until real life comes along and pops the bubble. Oh, we knew we were planning on having a cute bundle of love, baby Dexter. However, we didn't plan on this bundle of love coming with bills—doctor bills, hospital bills, food, diapers, clothes, shoes, more clothes, and more shoes. Not only was there bills just to keep baby Dexter supplied and alive, there were electric bills, car bills, and water bills—every month! Not to mention the daily personal, simple stuff for us like deodorant, laundry detergent, clothes (both regular and maternity), and shoes. It was an eye-opener and a hectic time.

Hectic. Wow. The storm brewing outside was hectic and scary. Trees were bending. The rain was pounding the yard away in little rivers of water—everywhere! I'm sitting here in the house listening to the weather person talk about hurricane force winds and how any-one in the affected path of the storm should take cover. Okay. Really scared now. Dexter was only five months old, so I am not liking this. All of a sudden, *blip*—the television went out along with the power in the house. I thought I was scared before. Now scared and sitting in a dark house with no streetlights so it's pitch dark outside. Listening to a raging storm outside—well, that takes scared to another level!

All of a sudden, Evan came running into the living room shout-ing, "Let's go!"

"Go? Go where?" I asked. "We can't go anywhere! Don't you hear that storm!" I shouted back at him. By this time, he's grabbed Dexter and covered him in a blanket and was trying to pull me through the house.

When we scuffled to the back door to step out on to the porch, I finally realized he was serious. So I pulled back and screamed above the storm, "What are you doing? We can't go out here—it's a storm." In my mind, I was thinking that he had lost his mind! We heard an eerie sound—kind of like a high soprano—wailing in the air.

He looked at me with big eyes and shouted, "That's it—we need to leave. It's almost here."

Well, at this point, I'm wet, confused, scared all at the same time. So blindingly, I followed him off the porch (after all, he has my baby!) across the yard and to the edge where there's a large manhole tunnel.

He shouted, "Follow me" while gesturing to the manhole.

"*What!*" I shouted.

He shouted back, "*Follow me!*"

"*No,*" I said. "We are not getting in there!"

He was insistent that I get down and crawl in the tunnel. My minds started to play a reel of trash, snakes, rats, and who knows what else, all in a matter of a nanosecond. Uhm, nope, not doing that. After more scuffling and disagreeing, we realized that the storm and wind had calmed down considerably. I grabbed my now soaking wet baby Dexter and ran back to the house, slipping and sliding through the yard.

When we are all three back in the house, I was somewhat concerned about what just happened. Did it really happen? What in the world was Evan thinking? Why was Evan thinking I would climb down in that tunnel? Is this something that we will need to do in the future?

I shouted at Evan, "What was that all about!"

He then proceeded to tell me that when there's a storm raging outside like that, we have to seek cover. He said that the wailing sound was the storm coming, and we couldn't stay in the house as it could get hit by the storm and collapse.

"*What?* I have never heard of such nonsense," I said.

He insisted that it's true. Well, all I know is that I'm not getting my baby nor myself in any tunnel. Evan will just have to build us an underground bunker or something out there in those woods 'cause this chick is not crawling into that tunnel…and that's final!

That summer came in blazing hot. I still have not forgotten this mind-boggling tunnel-in-a-storm incident. I made it a point to ask Evan about building something—a bunker—in case another storm like that comes through. He said that we'll be fine.

"Fine! Un-huh, my man. You had me out here in the middle of a storm, getting my Black girl no-permed hair wet with my infant child! You will build something, or you will get hurt."

In hindsight, something about my look or attitude must have registered because he did start building. That day, Evan started tearing off the outward wall facing of the garage and told me that he was going to close that part in so we'll have a large family room. He said that it's going to be big and solid and includes a half bath and laundry room. Now, at this point, I have not seen Evan build much… well, really, I haven't seen Evan build anything. Needless to say, I'm worried again. Did he just play me? I'm pretty sure he was supposed to build a safety bunker for us. Hmm, what if he tears something off and the whole house falls in? Oh my goodness, help, Lord.

# CHAPTER 2

# Lessons of the '80s

Well, thank You, Lord. Evan did indeed build that room with a half bath and laundry room included. Yes! It took a long time, but build it he did. Not only that, he went on to build a toddler bed for Dexter that was in the shape of a car! Yes, we had seen this bed in a magazine, and Evan said he was making Dexter one—he did, and it's really nice. After that, Evan is on a roll. He made a lovely bed headboard set for our bedroom. It had shelves on his and my side, as well as mirrors and a long shelf in the middle connecting to the sides. Beautiful.

At one point, Dexter even crawled up in the middle and sat on the shelf. He would take his toy truck with him and sit in there and laugh at himself in the mirror while playing. Cute. I have a picture of that somewhere in the house. I still have not forgotten about that storm issue.

I'm an unfit mother. I'm going to jail today. Oh my word, what do I do? I stand here on this cool October day outside of the doctor's office. Dexter and I had just left his well-check appointment, and I was walking out with another woman and her baby. As normal, she and I were discussing babies and how this doctor was better than another we both had previously visited. When we get to the car, I sat Dexter down and immediately got in to start the car up so it will be warmer before we get in. She and I finished our conversation. I put Dexter in his car seat along with the baby bag. I locked his door. When I got around to my driver's side, I realized he's now locked in, and I'm locked out.

Baby Dexter was only ten months old, and I locked him in the car! My immediate reaction was panic. Then, I quickly realized I've got to figure this out—fast! I rushed back into the office and told the receptionist what happened.

She said, "Don't worry, it happens more often than you think. I'll call 'John,' the local locksmith."

She did so, and he came right out. It was quite surprising how fast he got there. Do you know that he did not charge me anything? During this time, I was waiting to hear sirens and the police to come flying into the parking lot to accuse me of endangering a child. They never came. Hallelujah and thank You, Lord!

So naive. So young and dumb—both of us. Evan comes from a huge family. There are about five hundred of them and those are just his first cousins. Okay, that is not true, but you get my meaning. There are a whole bunch of them on both sides of his family! I remember vividly one Christmas when Dexter was about two years old. Evan and I had gone to his grandparents' house for Christmas dinner. Of course, when you have that many folks in one location, it's loud, funny, and a whole buffet of good old Southern home-cooked goodness.

One of Evan's relatives asked us what we had gotten Dexter for Christmas. We proudly stated how we stood in line at a store called Service Merchandise practically all night, in the cold, to get the newest video gaming system of the 80s and the games to go with it. Including the plastic orange gun that you used to shoot the ducks with when they flew up on the screen!

This relative then said, "What else?"

So we said that we got him shoes, clothes, and a coat. They had this look on their face as if thinking, "What in the world are these two doing with a baby?"

Aloud, we were then asked the question again but with emphasis, "*What else* did you get *the baby* to play with for Christmas?"

Aha! This time I understood. Only to realize in that same instant, we didn't get the baby anything to play with for Christmas. We got ourselves the latest and greatest gaming system. Whoa.

Thankfully, God knows what he is doing. Later that day when Evan and I arrived at my mom's house, Dexter had a ton of toys that were specifically tailored just for his age! He started playing with them immediately. I knew in that moment—okay, girl, you messed up.

Note to self: You really do have a child, and he's not a toy. Grow up and get it together. I'm pretty sure my mama knew all along that we had no idea what we were doing. Thank You, God, for mamas!

About the time in life we thought we had a handle on Dexter, life, and bills, along comes another bundle of love, baby Braden. Now we gotta refigure all of this out and try again. Lord, help!

Surely, if we're doing life with one child, we can do it again with two. I mean, how much harder can it get…right? We had no idea.

It got harder; life gets more interesting.

Now, previous to getting married, I've sat on side of the road many times during my high school years, awaiting for my dad to lovingly bring me the gas to put in my empty gas tank. He never said a word other than, "Gal, you got to keep gas in this car."

Occasionally when my car was out of gas, my dad was at work. It was at these times that my mom would call our neighbor, Mrs. Carmichael, to bring the gas. Oddly enough, I didn't want Mrs. Carmichael to bring it as she always came with a well-meaning lecture. "Young women need to keep gas in their car," "Keep your tank on full at all times," "Stop being lazy and put your gas in this car, baby," "It's dangerous to be out here with no gas," and many more that I was too lazy to listen to. After all, I was young and dumb but oh so confident. I alone knew what was best for me.

I say all that so you, the reader, will know that I have had many opportunities to sit on the side of roads awaiting help to come. However, when our car gave out, it was an entirely different thing. We were driving through a local town, and all of a sudden, the car started smoking! I've never seen this before. I yelled out for Evan to stop. We have got to get the children out because the car was going to blow up!

He looked at me as if I've lost my mind. He pulled over, looked under the hood, and said a bad word. While he's under the hood, I was unhooking baby seats and gathering everything I can and stuffing it into my purse and baby Braden's diaper bag. I mean, really, the car is going to blow up and I don't want any of our things to get blown to bits and pieces! I'm now standing outside with a child on each hip and a bag on each shoulder.

Evan looked from around the hood and told me to put that stuff up and get back in the car. He's walking to use the phone to call someone. (Yes, he had to walk as these were the days before cell phones existed).

"Get back in the car?" I asked.

"No way!" I said.

Evan then said, "Yes, just calm down. It's not going to blow up. We've got a blown head gasket."

I have no idea what that means, but I made him tell me a few times that all is well and that the car is not going to blow up while he's gone. Long story short, car was fixed, and we moved on to our next life adventure. If the song with the lyrics of "Jesus, Take The Wheel" had been out then, I'm pretty sure I would have been singing it.

After that, I had many more opportunities to sit on the side of the road such as:

- *Bald flat tires*—speaking of which, I wonder if anyone else besides me knows that if the street is too hot and you've got really bad tires, they will deflate. They will...ours did. True story.
- *Running out of gas*—not my fault this time. We just didn't have the money to buy gas. However, we were on our way to "borrow" some gas money from someone. They ended up bringing us the gas.
- *Tail pipe fell off the car*—in the road! We had to wait for traffic to clear, and Evan got it off the street, put it in the car, and away we went...very loudly. True story.

- *When the carburetor goes out*—I found out on this particular car emergency that you can put gas in this thing, and the car will start! Yes, I have no idea exactly how it works, but I saw Evan do it and the car started up. I'm not saying I recommend this, but I know it worked.

Harder still when the car can't be driven in the rain. I can't believe I'm telling this, but it is true. We had to be home before it would rain as the windshield washers didn't work on this particular vehicle. It's either be back home or stay where we were until the rain let up…completely. For everyone, we visited in the eighties and didn't leave when it was raining. We apologize. Yes, we loved you and hated to stay that long in your house, now you know why.

It got harder. When Evan can't get to work and the company decided they need to part ways. Speaks for itself. Harder still when you can't look for a job as there's no car. You live way out in the countryside, and there is no bus route. You can't call uber—it doesn't exist yet.

And it got harder. When the electric company turned off the lights. At this point, I must say that this is one of the reasons I have been known to shout thank you God in church. There's a song that says, "When I look back over my life and I think things over, I can truly say I have a testimony…" Yep, shouting time. Thank You, Lord!

In one particularly rough year, our lights would get turned off at least once every few months. Okay, maybe that's not quite true. But it sure felt like it! Evan has a "friend" who also has a "friend" who shall remain nameless. This friend was in the unethical business of assisting those who needed electricity. This one time, said friend would come by and wait a few hours after the electric company office closed. He would then trek outside to the power box and turn the lights back on! Me being me, I'm panicking and thinking we're about to go to jail and our children are going into some abused and misused child services department. So what do I do? Naturally, I'm calling out to God to help while I earnestly gather all the spreads and blankets. Then I proceeded to nail them to the walls around the windows so no one driving by at night can see that there were lights on in the house. Yes, I did that. Strange thing is that one of Evan's aunts came by one time and thought it was a great idea for me to hang the blankets on the windows! I don't know if she was saying it in a nice way that I was strange, or she actually thought it was a good idea. Needless to say, I couldn't take that anymore, so we had to let the "friend" carry on in that profession elsewhere. No more of that for us. Thank you, Lord, for your saving grace!

Speaking of lights getting turned off, one summer day, Evan and I were just merrily chilling and living our lives. Here again, the lights were scheduled to get disconnected that day. As usual, Evan was outside working on something. He's always got a project of some sort or another he's continually working at. I was in the house wondering when the electric company was going to arrive.

All of a sudden, I got fed up. I shouted, "Why God! Why does this keep happening! Help us, oh, God. Please help. We need money for the lights, for gas, and for grocery money. We need it right now." I remember falling down on the bed facedown and just lying there. Maybe five to ten minutes later, I heard a vehicle pull up in the yard. I didn't think anything about it as I've said before, my husband has a large passel of family, so it was not unusual for them to stop by at any time. Or it could be the electric company coming to do what they do…ugh!

Then I heard talking at the tree closest to our bedroom window. *That's strange*, I thought. I wondered why the electric company was over there by the tree. I got up and looked out the window. It's not the electric company truck. There's a stranger standing there talking to Evan. After a short time, they meandered back across the yard and to the driveway, out of my sight. I sat on the bed and suddenly Evan came rushing into the room.

"Guess what?" he says excitedly.

I have no idea.

He asked me, "Did you see that fellow outside?"

I replied, "Yes, I did."

He then told me that the man wanted to buy an old part that Evan just so "happened to have" sitting out there under that tree. The man offered him enough for the light bill, gas money for the car, groceries, *and* we had some money left for in the pocket—thank You, *Jesus*! You are talking about a girl shouting up in that house—hoowee! The interesting thing was Evan was intending to take that part to the junk yard. He just never got around to it. Look at God showing up and answering my prayer. Oh, I thank You, God. You better know that I had my behind at church on the following Sunday, paying my tithes. True story. Paying tithes. Wow. I just had a throwback thought on that.

> *"Bring all the tithes into the storehouse that there may be food in My house, And try Me now in this,"* says the Lord of hosts, *"if I will not open for you the windows of heaven and pour out for you such blessing, that there will not be room enough to receive it."* (Malachi 3:10)

One Sunday morning, I was getting ready for church thinking about how we had nothing for dinner that day. I knew I didn't get paid until Wednesday, so I was trying to put a meal together in my head while wishing I had money to go to the grocery store. I couldn't find anything I wanted to wear, and it was getting late. This was one of the few times Evan was actually ready to go before me. In a huff of exasperation, I chose a colorful shirt that had a pocket on the upper left-hand side and a black skirt I hadn't worn in years. Out the door we flew to church.

This particular Sunday, as the usher's team were coming forth to take up the collection, the pastor was telling this Bible story found in Mark 12. *Jesus teaches the disciples that the woman gave more than the rich. The poor woman, as a widow, would have had no source of income after her husband's death. Therefore, two small copper coins were all she had, and she offered them to God.* I knew I didn't have any money to put in the collection plate other than the 17¢ in my purse. I remember talking to God and saying, "Okay, Lord, you heard the

Bible verse the pastor just read. So I'm going to take you at your word and see what happens."

I put the change in the collection plate and got up to go get some water from the fountain in the vestibule of the church. As I bent over to slurp the water, I heard a crinkling in the pocket of the shirt. I stood back up and reached into the pocket and pulled out a $50.00 bill. What? I immediately did a little shout right there at the water fountain. Thank You, God!

It got harder. When the well water we were using started running cloudy…oh my goodness. True to my nature, I panicked. What in the world was going on with the water! I've never seen this before. We're going to die. The water looked dingy! Turns out that when it doesn't rain for a while, the water in the well gets low, and this is what it comes out of the pipes as—dingy-looking, cloudy water.

I remember standing in the kitchen saying, "Oh no! We are getting on the city water line. My children are not drinking cloudy water!" After Evan and I found out how much it was going to cost to have a waterline installed and for the county to come out and install the pipes and hook us up to the line, *well*, let's just say a little cloudy water every now and then didn't hurt us. Thankfully, there was also bottled water at the local grocers. Praise God that our sons are blessed and doing fine and healthy today.

# CHAPTER 3

# The '90s—Walking in Favor

It's a new day living in the 90s now and things were going our way. Life was great, and things were looking up. We have moved up and are living a pretty good life. We now have a reliable car. In fact, Evan was out with my brother and his brothers fishing right now, and they went in our car. We're both working—yes! Kids were healthy…wait. Braden turned three years old this summer. He's in the floor playing with his cousins.

Out of the blue, he got up, walked across the floor, and climbed up in my lap. Then he proceeded to have a full-blown seizure—eyes rolled back in his head, spittle foaming at the mouth, and body shaking uncontrollably. I screamed. My brother's girlfriend yelled at me to hand her the baby and to go get a spoon. I did so and then proceeded to run one-quarter mile in the rain up the street to my husband's cousin's house asking for help to get baby Braden to the hospital.

We arrived at the hospital. The verdict was that Braden had a fever of 103 degrees which caused the said seizure. All is well and thank God that has never happened again. Oh, and did I mention that while I was running, I ran out of my house shoes, and to this day, those shoes are still not found? When it rains, I still wait to see if I will see my shoes in a rain puddle. I really liked those shoes.

My takeaway lessons from that hair-raising time still remains today. I will always have a variety of meds in the house. I will always have a phone in the house.

The lighter moments during this time was that Evan is still building the things we need with his hands. Lord, thank You for blessing Evan with this talent—who knew? He's now working on a kids' ride-along-car for the boys—they can both fit in it. It's made of wood and painted what he called Chevrolet blue. I must admit, I am impressed, again, with my husband. A lot of times when Evan was outside working, the boys will be out there alongside of him, playing with his tools and working on their car. It's so cute.

This was also the time when I developed a love for fresh fish. Kids were getting older—they want food! Fast food is fine on the occasional visit. It is not recommended as part of a daily health plan. We have two growing boys—they eat a lot of food. Thankfully, Evan is a fisherman all the way to his bone marrow. He loves fish and even eats the sardines in the can. I haven't quite mastered that one yet.

When you are hungry, you will try what you may not normally eat and find that it is quite delicious. I learned this lesson the belly-rumbling way. We were residing on property that had a creek and several fishing ponds were all around. Whenever we didn't have meat for dinner, guess what Evan always came home with? Fish! Many meals I've made with fish were as follows:

- Crispy fried crappie—one of my favorites, delicious.
- Catfish stew—thanks to his grandmother Smith for that recipe. I never thought I'd eat that, but who knew it would be so good?
- Flounder and rainbow trout—delicious.
- Bream fish nuggets—Evan once caught one of these fish that was so big that he split it with his brothers and their families. We're talking about six adults and six kids. That was a *huge* fish.

One of the first meals made with the meat from that fish were fish nuggets that fed all of us! I believe someone made reference to Jesus feeding the crowd while we were all sitting around eating that night. Thank You, Lord, for the feast because all of us were broke and hungry that night!

To this current day, both of our sons are avid fishermen like their dad. Their wives will tell you that they can "smell" a pond to go fishing in. Just like their dad, they keep a fishing pole in their cars… just in case. It is in their bloodline.


Men. Husbands. Fathers. They are great people. They will make you want to kill them. Really. Today, I am so annoyed with Evan. I just look at him and think, *What in the world is he thinking?* It was a beautiful and hot summer day. Evan wanted to go to the creek on our property and have some fun in the water.

"Great idea," I said to him.

So we gathered the boys, some of their water toys, and fishing poles. Off we all went across the yard, over the field, and down the hill to the creek. In my little naive mind, I was assuming that we're going to sit alongside the water with feet dangling in. Dexter and Braden will be playing along the edge of the water, splashing and having fun. Evan will be standing somewhere close by, fishing. That is exactly what happened for about thirty minutes.

After a while, Evan came and started playing with them. *Then* he picked Dexter up and threw my baby in the deepest part of the creek!

"What are you doing?" I yelled. Then I almost strangled on my saliva as he picked Braden up and does the same thing to him. He goes out to them and was right there with them as they each came up and he's letting them struggle and swim! As my eyes were seeing this, my mouth was screaming, "*No!* Help them!"

Evan was actually laughing. I'm going to kill him just as soon as I get my hands on him. It took a good full minute or two for my brain to realize that both Braden and Dexter were laughing… Yes, laughing! They were fine, and I couldn't believe my eyes. They were actually trying to swim—what? Well, praise God. I didn't have to commit murder today, but I will never forget this Evan. Never.

The 90s were also a time for Evan and myself to come into some realizations. Guess what? If you actually put money in the bank, save it, and you will see that it draws interest. Even better, if you put money in your 401(k), the company will actually match it, and it all saves up! As long as the market is doing good—we're doing good! We also learned not to watch it all the time. That will drive you batty watching how stocks and bonds go up and down.

There really is something to be said about not watching your money in the market. It's only for the brave. Or in our case, desperate for change to happen. It's pretty cool once you get the hang of it—we like seeing things grow. There were also these catalogs of paper in the Sunday papers called coupons. You cut them out, collect them, and go shopping. Give them to the cashier when you checkout, and you save money on your groceries. If you're really good at it, you can save quite a few dollars on your grocery bill. I've even learned about saving money on gas. Drive a five-speed? When going downhill, let the car coast…all the way down.

Know something better? Have the owner at the neighborhood country store remember Evan's dad from when he was younger. This man would let us run up a tally at his store to get anything—gas, groceries, cooked food (they sold bologna meat and freshly made hotdogs), canned food, medicine, diapers, or whatever we needed. I've said many "God bless them" prayers for this man and his wife. They were a true blessing to us.

Whenever Evan got the money to pay his bill, he would go by there and pay it then turn around and start another running tally. It was many years later that Evan went into that same store and the man was there and said, "Y'all must be doing pretty good. I don't see you anymore."

My response was, "Yes, we are so blessed." It felt great to buy from him and pay for it on the spot.

In all the years of Evan having to fix our various car parts, he was always learning more about cars and fixing other people's cars. I always knew both of our sons were paying attention and hanging around outside with him. It never really hit home to me that they were actually learning something about cars until we were on a trip in Washington, DC.

I drove my white Chevrolet from South Carolina to DC in the summer of year 2000, me and the boys. For some reason that year, Evan didn't go with us. Anyway, we got to my sister's, Tatiana's, house there in DC, and there is an oil leak under the car. Do you know Dexter got out there and fixed that leak enough to get us over to the station to have it fixed? I honestly don't know what he did, but all the other guys were pretty impressed with it.

Since that time, both Dexter and Braden have made me proud with their inherited skills from their father. If nothing else, their families will always have a car running and be able to have fresh fish on the dinner table. They just need to remember if they're running low on gas, let the car coast on the downhill.

It was also during this time that I realized more ways to save money. At one point I saw a commercial advertising a special on entrance to an out of state amusement park. If you bring a bag of this particular name brand soda cans, one person can get in free with a certain number of cans! Oh, you know it was on then. I started collecting all these soda cans I could get my hands on. Evan, a.k.a. doubting Thomas, didn't think we could all four get in with our plastic grocery bags of empty Cola cans. I knew we could.

Since it was rather far-fetched, I called right before we left the house to be sure.

The agent said, "Yes, that's all you need, the cans."

I even wrote down her name so when I got to the ticket office, I could have them call her if there are any problems. After all, we were on a very limited income, and I was learning to find all kinds of ways to do things and enjoy life with little to no money in my pocket.

That summer, I packed up our lunches, coolers, and snacks and away we went on I-85 to the amusement park. We paid and parked the car and took the shuttle up to the ticket gates. Of course, it's summer, so the lines are long. I don't want to wait in line to see if this is going to work. So I stopped an agent and asked about the entrance with these name brand soda cans. He had no idea what I was talking about.

In the background, I could hear Evan's mumbling, "I told you this wouldn't work. We came way out here for nothing."

I tried the next person who directed me to someone else who pointed me to another set of ticket windows located off the beaten path of where everyone else was waiting. No line over there. By this time, it felt like everyone was looking and watching us. No matter what, these soda cans are our tickets, and I'm getting in this theme park today.

After the agent counted the empty soda cans, it turned out that I had given her too many. She asked if I wanted them back.

I said, "No, keep it for the next person who may not have enough." Cans accepted and hands stamped, we were now in the theme park. Let the fun begin! We actually came back that same summer with more bags of soda cans, and this time, I knew where to go to get in. Again, we got in with no problem. Both times we had a great, family fun-filled day! Evan was quite surprised. I remember him asking me how I knew about that deal. I told him I saw it on TV. Funny thing though, no one else seems to have seen that commercial. Must be what's called a God thing. Thank You, God!

The best way to save money? Grow your food yourself. Evan is a farmer, born, bred, and raised. I knew this fact when we were married, however, I didn't fully appreciate how much so until we had these two baby boys and needed more food. One fine sunny day, he came walking in the house with corn, green beans, and pears. Yes, pears! I love all fruits, and when I saw our first bounty, I was hooked!

Every year, you can find him out there tilling the soil and planning whatever's on his mind that year to plant. I mean everything from peppers (three kinds) excluding ghost peppers. We heard those will mess up the taste of everything else in the garden, so we don't bother with them. Every vegetable you can think of, even a few we just experimented with, eggplant and broccoli were the most fun and beans. Oh my goodness, seems every year we have so many beans that I am giving them away to any and all who wants them. I even learned from a coworker that you can eat them raw! Yes, I gave her a bag of fresh beans, and she proceeded to eat them out of the bag. She said they were great tasting. Who knew?

Of course, the fruit is my favorite—watermelons, cantaloupes, peaches, apples, and muscadines. Yeah baby. This farming thing is pretty cool and great on the purse. Not to mention, I can freeze most everything that comes from this garden—tomatoes, okras, corns, tons of beans, squash, and peas. Thank You, Lord!

# CHAPTER 4

# Blessings and Angelic Encounters

If you haven't figured it out by now, I'm what they call a scaredy-cat. I will do devilment with the best of them. However, I do not want to get in trouble. Thus, the season of me discovering that you can write checks but you must have money in the bank! Checks are not magic. You can't write one and then "hope" the money will just appear in the account before the check hits. I learned that in this season. If the check doesn't clear the bank, you must then go back to the vendor and make good on that check. Trust me on this. It really helps even further if you pay your tithes and get a budget journal. Write it down! If you have no money, do not write the check. Of course, in this new age, I don't know many who still write checks. They are written by some, just not as much as back when I was writing them. Thank, God, for growth, wisdom, and His mercy!

Funnily enough, none of the four—yes, four—vendors I wrote checks to are still in business today. Maybe they all went bankrupt due to people like me just writing checks like they were billionaires… Well, in my case, *twentydollaraires*.

This is the season I realize my children may be snobs. Yes, I said it—snobs. For some reason, they do not want to shop at our local, very well-known used goods store. Seriously, boys? Granted I don't shop here often—okay, rarely. However, Easter is a couple of months away, and they need suits. Someone told me that I could get some really good deals here, so we are going to check it out.

I'm always in the market for saving money. We're in this used goods store, and Dexter was having an attitude saying he doesn't want any of these clothes. Naturally, now Braden was trying to copy him and had an attitude as well, saying he doesn't want anything out of here as well. They are serious.

Braden wants to go the mall to Montgomery Ward. In hindsight, I don't know why we always shop there but that was our store. We would always park on that end of the mall and shop there first before heading out into the other mall stores. Anyhow, after hearing him say this, I realize there is a big difference in the two stores and that is probably why they didn't want to shop there. I, however, realize I am not about to write a check for some suits they are going to sooner rather than later grow out of. Been there, done that, and I am not doing it again.

Well, after about twenty minutes of fruitless searching, off to Wards we go. They each get some black pants, white shirts, and pastel-colored ties. Done. It was all on the sale rack—thank You, Lord! Who knew some twenty years later, that same local, very well-known used goods store would be the fashionable place that everyone shops at today! Makes me wonder if Dexter and Braden shop there now. Ha!

Speaking of the age when checks were an often used monetary transaction, we actually have money built up in the bank at this time. I was asked to usher on a church program that would be held one Sunday afternoon. After asking around, I found out that all ushers needed to wear white. Yikes, I don't have a white dress to wear. I don't have anything that's white. I need to go shopping.

By this time in life, I've gotten into the habit of continuous prayer. Evan and I pulled up to the mall—yes, we're at the mall again. Evan decided to wait in the car with the boys. They don't have a men's automotive nor a fishing and hunting department in this store. Before getting out, I sat in the car and prayed to God that I can find something under $100.00 to wear for this church program.

After perusing the racks, I found the perfect white dress, sheer white hosiery and shoes…totaling right at $125.00. I sighed and headed to register to check out. To my surprise, the entire order was $68.00! All of the items were on season clearance sale, and I didn't know it… thank You, God. Wait. This gets better.

The saleslady rings me up, I wrote the check for the $68.00. She took it and did her thing with the register then stapled the check to my receipt and gave it back to me…strange. She proceeded to bag up my hosiery and shoes, put my dress in a garment bag, smiled at me, thanked me for shopping that store, and told me to have a great day. Then she gave me both bags. I'm confused… I thought she was supposed to keep the check.

This was back in the day before stores started running the checks at the registers. She had nothing to run…just some push buttons on the big register on the counter. I watched my account for a whole year awaiting that check to clear! It never did. I kid you not! I even asked others about it, and they all said she messed up. Apparently so. This store is still in business today at the mall. It's one of mine and Evan's favorite stores, and we still patronize it today. Thank you, God, for your grace covering me.

Summer of 1998. It's Sunday afternoon—a beautiful sunny day. I'm berating myself because I woke up late today and didn't make it to church—I overslept. I tried justifying it by telling myself that I have a very good reason. Evan and I hosted our families with a huge yard cookout on yesterday. As usual, we had a ton of people, cars in the yard and on the street as well, music for dancing, blow-up pools with water splash fun, volleyball and badminton games going, and grills blazing with food for days and just overall a family good time. I was exhausted by the time the last person left around 1:47 a.m., so I went to bed.

Evan and the boys stayed up a little longer and cleaned up what was left of the firecrackers display. Thus, we all overslept. So I find myself walking out the door headed for the backyard just looking for whatever tidbit someone may have left behind. I have found that someone always forgets something or mistakenly leaves something behind—baby bags, umbrellas, purses, a dish, a favored toy, etc. Today, I looked up and saw a pretty and colorful jump rope stretched out across the backyard.

*Wow*, I think to myself. *That jump rope is so pretty.* Just look at all the colors in it—yellow, white, orange, black, and a pretty coral color. I don't remember anyone playing with it, but I wasn't everywhere, so I guess I missed it. I headed over to pick it up so I can put it away for safekeeping for whoever calls to ask if we've seen it. All of a sudden, the jump rope moved.

*"Argh!"* I screamed and continued to scream as I ran back into the house. Evan knows this scream. He knows to get the shovel or shotgun and kill the beast. That darn snake just ruined my beautiful day. I'm pissed now. I couldn't even go sit outside and enjoy the day. Nerves were shot. Skin was crawling. I really wanna say a bad word right now. *Crapdabbit!*

Up until this point, we were doing life our way and praising God with a tepid relationship. Most times, it was on a low simmer with the occasional fire popper. It wasn't until I started going to revival on a regular basis and really digging into the Word that my thirst for God started to increase. When I tell you God started showing up and showing out in our lives, wow, talk about praying to God for a car and suddenly, Evan showed up on my job with one that was practically given to us. Yes, it happened, and the price was ridiculously low.

Another time I was going to the restroom at work and just talking to God about our life and asking Him for a raise only to come out of that restroom to a note on my desk to go to the director's office. I got to the office and was offered a promotion and a retro raise! Yes, it happened. That same company later went bankrupt.

Out of 250 plus employees, they decided to keep the business going with a handful of (20) employees. Guess who was one of those 20 employees kept? Yes, me all the way to the final day which occurred three years later. That really happened. Thank you God.

During this time, there were several companies and potential buyers coming through looking at the property and offices. That was not unusual. However, one such time, the other two ladies in the office were in a fit to give these particular guys their résumé. They were from a strange sounding company I never heard of. I wasn't interested. One lady especially kept bugging me to print out my résumé to give to them before they left.

At one point, she even said, "Hurry, Aretha!" After a lot of "killing time" and hoping they would leave before I printed it out, I finally gave it to them. I was seriously hoping and thinking they wouldn't call. I thought nothing more about it.

At this particular office, there was a closet of office supplies and extra odds and ends from the office. I would often find myself using this closet to pray to God or talk to Him about something going on in the office that I needed His advice on. On my final day at this company, I went into this closet to talk to God. I remember telling Him that this is my last day in the office. I'm going to take this lovely severance check they've given me and travel with my sons and nieces to see the world. We've got family all over the world, so I'm going to take the kids and go see them. Maybe start in Germany and work my way to Alaska. After that—who knows. I told God that if He wants me to do something differently, I will but He's going to have to tell me. If God wants me to work, then all I ask three things: (1) more money, (2) stay in the downtown area I currently work in, and (3) make it a better and more fun place than the office I'm about to leave.

Wow. When I left the office that day, I went to a local storage facility to pay the bill for my aunt's items she had in storage. As I parked, I saw what looked like a homeless man with a grocery store buggy full of what I thought was junk. I remember thinking, *that homeless fellow looks very clean.* He had the prettiest eyes—kind of amber, clear colored. His hair was gorgeous curly locks with a deep, rich skin tone. I reached into the passenger seat to grab my purse while also opening the driver's door. As I turned and looked up to get out, there he stood.

For some reason, I was not afraid. I actually got out and stood up with the door between us. I was between the car and the door.

He looked at me and said, "Ma'am, I don't know you. You don't know me. God sent me to tell you He heard your prayer today, and He wants you to take the job based on scripture."

Before I knew it, I had shut the car door and grabbed him and was hugging him. I was crying and thanking him. That man and I stood out there in the hot July sun talking about God for about two hours. Oh my goodness, we had the best fellowship time. Eventually, I made it in to pay my aunt's bill. It was only then I realized I did not get that man's name.

When I got home that afternoon, I went into my home office, sat down in my chair, and pulled up my computer to check random e-mails. I saw one from that strange company I had given my résumé to. *Oh*, I thought to myself, *they are probably telling me thanks but no thanks*. Which was fine with me. I was going to wait for the job based on scripture that God was sending my way.

Well, I opened the email and the very first thing I read was the header. It said, "*Walk in wisdom toward others redeeming the time. Let your speech always be with grace, seasoned with salt that you may know how you ought to answer* (Colossians 4:5–6, NIV)."

*What?* It's a good thing I was sitting down as I would have fallen over had I not. Once I got over that shock, I read further down the official contract offering me a job. I've now been with them, on assignment from God, for over a decade now. To God be the glory!

My prayer life took a steep curve and before I knew it, I was praying like never before. Help me, Lord! Teen years of boys, and I am not ready. This is the season I stopped going into our sons' bedroom to straighten things up to my satisfaction. I thought I was a praying woman before. Never as much as I did during the teen years of boys. Wow.

Take for instance the day I found some man-geared reading material in one of the bedrooms. What? It was during the school week, and I was home cleaning house. I was cleaning the room. I lifted the covers off the bed to change them—and *whomp*, there it was!

*Oh no, this cannot be*, I thought. He's only fifteen. My heart was beating in my chest so hard right now. Well, I went running out the house across the backyard to whisper to Evan of what I just found. The first thing he did was to look at me as if I've lost my mind.

He then asked me, "Why are you whispering?"

"Well, I don't know. It just seemed like the thing to do," I said.

He then started laughing and told me that was great news.

"How is it great news?" I asked. "We're not talking about the Bible here—that's the great news. Did you not understand? I said I found this magazine in his bed. Aren't you concerned?"

He proceeded to tell me that no, he's not concerned and that it's great news and for me to leave it at that.

"Seriously? That's all you've got to say about this."

He said, "Yes, now put it back and leave the room alone."

I did put it back and made a note to myself to not clean their rooms again. They are officially on their own. I can't take it. Jesus, handle your children!

The time I saved one of our sons' lives, he and I were having a very heated discussion on life and the choices we make. I came within an inch of throwing one of my dining room chairs at him! The only reason I didn't is that I am very fond of that dining room set. Well…that and the fact that I'm pretty sure Jesus stepped in right on time. He is an on-time God. Hallelujah!

Just when I think I can move on, I now find the need to make an investment in a case of lotion for my knees. Apparently, they will be ashy for some years to come. Now Braden comes along and says he wants to join the US Army. Talk about getting weak and suddenly falling to one's knees…and it wasn't because I was slain in the spirit! Those were five of the longest years spent in continual talks and prayers to God. Thus, the need to invest in lotion. All the time I spent in prayer on my knees resulted in what we in the south called ashy skin, meaning the skin looks rough and dry. Shine it up!

In the beginning at one point, I was a little put out with God. Why does my child have to be the one to go serve this messed up country? The answer was, "Why not your child? Mine actually died for you *and* your child."

Okay, so I shut up and said, "Thank You, Jesus. Have your way, Lord." Here again, I chose to take the high road thanking God for his safety, thanking God that he was getting opportunities to see the world, thanking God that he was getting life experiences, thanking God that Evan and I were seeing him grow up and hearing the boy becoming a man in our conversations. "Thank You, God, for your son who gave his life for the sons you gave to us to raise. I will not complain."

---

# CHAPTER 5

# Satan, Get under My Feet and Stay There!

Fast forward a couple thousand prayers, both Dexter and Braden were now grown and moved out. It's just Evan and I. There was a spirit pressing on me, and I did not like it. I wished I could say it's because we're empty nesters. Sadly, that's not it. I had a painful truth to face and fight. How to fix it…only God knows.

It's Saturday and raining outside. I was in a dark place. Why, oh, why? I was walking through the house looking and thinking. Strangely, a moment of suicide entered my thoughts and scared the daylights out of me! What! The devil you say—get outta here! It's not that bad…right? I am stronger than this…right? I can conquer this…right? When did this happen? I am thankful yet ashamed. I am blessed yet embarrassed. I am favored yet depressed. How can this be? Why should this be? When did this happen? How long must it go on? How is it possible to shout and praise God on Sunday (or any day of the week) and then must tepidly walk through my house? Why must I have thoughts to feed and bless others with a kitchen full of food yet can invite no one over? Don't even think about knocking on this door and asking for something as simple as a saltine cracker. That thought alone sends my mind into a whirlwind of panic. What if someone does knock? I can't let them in here. All hell would break loose.

We've been married for a few decades. History has done its damage, and it cannot be undone. Things are broken that cannot be fixed. There are holes that no amount of Spackle can close. Duct tape can't hold this. Super glue is useless. The question remains—why?

Honestly, I know the answer to all these questions and more. It is one thing. Yes, one thing. I have the nerve to want to give in to despair and depression over it. I have the audacity to sit here in this chair and let my tears fall as fast and as hard as the rain is falling outside. I am sitting in the blessing. A wonderful heritage left to my husband by his hard-working parents. We have been so busy living this life and squeezing every bit of fun and enjoyment out of our lives that we are guilty. I've fallen into this dark pit of guilt because we let this home built with love fall in around us while we were enjoying the fruits of it.

Somewhere along the way, we forgot to kill the termites. You know, the pesky things you see flying outside every now and then. However, they were doing a terrible (or wonderful for them) job on the foundation of our home. So much so that it is now too late to have it fixed.

What have we taught our kids? I'm always talking about the Lord this and the Lord that. I feel as if they are looking and saying, "Well, Mama, how come the Lord didn't fix this?" I have failed. I feel as if my husband's parents are looking and saying, "Well, look at what they did to what we left them." I am embarrassed as I am now one of "those people" who talk one way yet live another way. I do not want to be that person. We will come out of this for the better. I just don't know how yet. God gets all the glory for what He is doing. I walk by faith not by sight. Word.

Thank You, Lord. I feel a revival in my spirit. There's a saying that confession is good for the soul. I believe it—just typing these paragraphs out helps me to feel better. As I've often heard quite a few pastors say, "I feel my help coming on now! Hallelujah!"

We are now grandparents and have two daughters-in-love. Yes, love. Surprisingly so. I didn't think I could make room for anyone to share my sons' love. Wrong. I actually love these ladies. They treat my sons well and with respect. I can see growth in them. They have dreams and plans. They love me! Oh, I could have tried to pick out the women for our sons to marry and did what I would have considered an excellent job…at the time. That is not what happened—at all. Both my sons picked out their future wives without my help. They married them and went on with their lovely lives. They call for help when they want prayers over whatever decisions are about to be made. They call to share their joys, so we rejoice together over whatever life has bestowed on them. We have three rambunctious, growing, and inquisitive grandsons. Still no granddaughters. I declare at least one to be in our future…lol! Oh, and the lovely women I had picked out in my mind? Let's just say God really does know what's best for all of us. He does not need our help with His master plan for our lives. Thank You, God.

# CHAPTER 6

# A New Level of Tests and Faith

WARNING: To you, the reader, remember: this is my diary of bits that I am sharing. My thoughts, feelings, and reality. From this point on, things may get a little graphic or be "too much" for you. If that is you, just skip to the last chapter of my book, and know I appreciate your taking the time to have read this far. I love you and continue to pray for you. You have no idea!

> The LORD is my shepherd, I lack nothing.
> He makes me lie down in green pastures,
> he leads me beside quiet waters,
> he refreshes my soul.
> He guides me along the right paths
> for his name's sake.
> Even though I walk
> through the darkest valley,[a]
> I will fear no evil,
> for you are with me;
> your rod and your staff,
> they comfort me.
> You prepare a table before me
> in the presence of my enemies.
> You anoint my head with oil;

my cup overflows.
Surely your goodness and love will follow me
all the days of my life,
and I will dwell in the house of the Lord
forever. (Psalm 23 NIV)

The year 2017 is our year. We gave got plans and no issues to stop us. The best-laid plans…welcome 2017! Can't wait to see what's next!

It's February 2017. For some reason, that I do not know, I was being led to take the week of May 8 through the 12 off for vacation. I have nothing planned. Strange. Normally, if I'm taking an entire week for vacation, then there is something going on, and usually it involves me traveling with my family. By boat, car, plane, train or something. This time, it's strange. I have nothing planned to do. Even my coworkers were asking what I had planned for that week or where is my family headed off at this time. My answer is the same for everyone. I'm planning to sit home on my porch, drink my favorite Cranapple and grape juice drink, and read tons of books while enjoying the May sunshine. This feels odd to my own ears. Why am I being led to take this week off?

It was also during this time that I was beginning to notice my hair. It's falling out! It began slowly with a bit here and a bit there. Now, it's a handful here and a handful there, yikes!

In early April 2017, my doctor has now exhausted all tests for this mysterious hair loss. My beautician has tried all she knows. Skin dermatologist has run every test possible. No one can figure out why my hair was falling out. My doctor then decides she wants to go ahead and do my yearly mammogram. I have it done and as usual, I receive a letter in the mail wanting me to get a second appointment. Whatever. I'm not going to do it until I have time…maybe later this fall. I go through this every year. They want to take another look, and it always turned out to be nothing.

I'm at work in late April and I get a call from the doctor's office, asking if I'd scheduled my mammogram recheck. I said not yet. The aide then proceeded to tell me they'd made my recheck appointment for me, and it was the next day! I'm like, "Really, can I just call back and reschedule it for later?"

She said, "No, the doctor wants you to be there tomorrow at the offices in Greenville."

So I said, "Sure, I'll be there," while thinking to myself about how things are changing at Dr. Napoor's office. They are really working to stay on top of us patients. Her office is in another city, so I just figured it was nice of them to schedule my appointment here in the city I work in. It's convenient for me to drive there to this closer office. At least that's where my train of thought was.

So I finally get to the appointment. Of course, by this time, my thinking has changed. I started thinking, *What is going on? Could this be more serious than what I've been thinking? Why the sudden rush to have a second appointment?* Dr. Napoor's office has never done this before. My name was called, and I was led to the little lovely "boob closet." Once again, I've undressed, donned the breast gown, and opened the front and was having my breasts poked, crushed, and prodded in this machine that is determined to flatten them to a pancake. All the while, I'm supposed to be a contortionist, holding my breath and not moving. Oh my goodness, I see stars!

What seemed like forever only took about fifteen minutes. Thankfully, I'm done. I'm now scheduled for an appointment for the following Thursday for a biopsy. I was told that there are some "suspicious-looking spots" on my mammogram, aka "clusters of calcifications." I walked out of the doctor's office in a daze. When I got home that afternoon, I decided to sit out in the sunshine and read. To my amazement, I realize I'm now dying! I've got a foreign breast disease normally found in the outbacks of Ocutumbawac. It's true because when I googled my symptoms on WebMD, that's exactly what it said!

Okay, all jokes aside. Reality check. I went to my biopsy appointment and was not really sure what that involved. I was led to a little room where the mammogram closets are for changing your clothes. Once again, I found myself disrobing in the cold closet and putting on the lovely tops they give you. The wonderful nurse then took me into a softly lit room, which I thought was strange.

They're about to cut into my boob, shouldn't we have more light? Like a *lot* of light for cutting purposes! Apparently not. The nurse then proceeded to tell me everything that was about to take place, including the strange table I was looking at. I was told to take my time and lay my face down on this hard slab of table that would be mechanically raised or lowered. Seriously, this table had no cushion whatsoever; just a hard slab of plastic. In the process of lying down, you stick your boobs into the two round holes that were cut into the table. The side of your face lies on a pillow and your hands are down by your side. Yikes. I like to see where my boobs are, at all times. This is not the most comfortable feeling.

Once the doctor came into the room, he gave some very soft-spoken, comforting words. I assume they were comforting. I'm not really sure since I couldn't see him and I was more concerned about my boobs that were now hanging in the hole of this weird table. I feel pretty confident I made some kind of mumbling response to his comments. The nurse then proceeded to raise the table and I felt some pressure on the boob they were about to work on. The pressure is the stabilizer paddles they used to hold the breast in place. I pretty soon found out the paddles are also to keep you locked down and from slapping someone when they stick you with the needle to numb the breast! Ouch! This does not feel good. Eventually, ahhh sweet relief when the numbing meds kick in.

I now understand this soft light effect. It's to help keep you calm. The doctor and nurse were under the table doing their thing. I was starting to somewhat relax and found myself drooling on the pillow. *Ewwww.* Really girl! *Close your mouth.* I don't get to fall into a deep sleep as every few minutes, the nurse was soothing my shoulder and back and making positive comments like "You're doing great," "We're almost done," etc.

Eventually, they are done. The doctor makes more comments that I just cannot remember what he said. Why do I continue to tune him out but listen so attentively to the nurse? Weird. My next appointment is two days later to get an MRI.

Okay. That Monday happened to be the first day of my scheduled vacation week. You know, the one I had no idea what I would be doing that week. I find this fact interesting yet alarming. Knowing God, I now feel He is up to something, and I also feel like I don't want to know what it is. I'm here for the MRI. I've never had one before so to say I was intrigued is an understatement. I was watching all the female staff involved in this process, trying to read their faces. Of course, being as well trained as they are, they didn't reveal a thing. They were outgoing and friendly. One nurse in particular made it a point to explain everything that was going to happen and what the machines were going to do and sound like. She patiently answered all my questions…and believe me, I had quite a few.

Here again, I was led into another little closet to don the dreaded breast gown. No jewelry whatsoever is allowed. It's cold in this one! The nurse then proceeded to tell me about the procedure. While she was doing so, I noticed a big door with black and yellow caution tape on the floor outside the entrance to the room There's also a radiation warning sign posted with a skull. Whoa. What? The nurse noticed me and stopped talking. She looked me in the eyes and asked if I was alright. My reply to her was "of course I'm not alright. Looks like you're about to take me through a war zone–restricted area." She laughed and continued her explanation saying she loved my sense of humor. Huh. Carrying on with her explanations is the fact that I'll have to wear earplugs. I'm told the machine will be making loud noises off and on throughout the procedure. Interesting. I don't think I'll need them but okay, we'll see.

I'm also poked with a needle and given an IV drip in my arm as partway through the MRI, I'll be given dye from the machine which will flow into me through the IV.

She wanted to verify if I'm only allergic to penicillin. "Anything else?" she asks.

I reply, "Yes, I'm allergic to this entire process. Can we just forget about it and avoid it altogether? You got a pill I can just take to make it all go away?"

She replies, "Oh, sweetie, I wish we did."

I say, "Oh well, let's do this."

We then went into this room with a huge circular contraption of a table with openings on both ends. Here again, I am told that I'll need to hike my legs up like I'm getting on a horse. Then lay on my stomach, facedown, with my head in the headrest and breasts in the holes. I laughingly think to myself, *These medical folks love these breast holey tables*. At least this table is more comfortable as it has cushiony padding on it.

This time, my hands went in front of me and were loosely clasped together. Once I was in place, they hooked up the line from the machine into my IV post. I decided I would keep watching this line to see what color the dye will be. I was told that once the machine starts, I cannot move and do heavy breathing, and I have to hold very still for the next thirty-five minutes. Thank goodness, I don't need to use the restroom. I prayed that I don't need to sneeze or have an itch.

All right, the MRI has now started and this machine is making some strange noises. Oh, this isn't bad at all. About five minutes in, I'm ready to move. Wait, I can't move. Think about something else to distract myself. Maybe the ABCs…not working. How about praying…don't want to pray. Then I notice the inverted mirror that lets me see in/around the room while lying face down on this table. Now that's cool. I'm looking in that mirror and checking out the room. I can even see the staff behind that darkened window over there! I wonder how much time has passed, I'm ready to get out of here. Oh no. Am I getting a feeling of claustrophobia? Yep. Time to speak to myself, "Breathe, girl, but not too deep. You are not claustrophobic. You are not enclosed. Your feet and hands are free. You're in an open room lying in this huge machine with no barriers." I decide to just start thanking God for this season he's got me in. I don't know why He's doing this, but I'm determined to give Him the glory. There's the song that pops up: "If you can use anyone Lord, you can use me." Apparently, I've got a job or mission to do and this is part of it. I will succeed, and he will be proud of me. I almost start humming the song, but I remember I'm not supposed to move. So back to daydreaming. For some reason, I think about the TV lady who says, "Ain't nobody got time for that!" This makes me smile. Does that count as moving? I hope not. I had better turn my thoughts elsewhere as I don't want to have to start all over and do this again simply because of a smile movement.

A thought: Isn't it past time for the dye? I didn't see anything. The line was still clear plastic. One of the nursing staff said something into the room's microphone. I have no idea what she said, so I'll just continue to lie here. I can't move and run the risk of screwing this MRI up just to start all over again. Nope, not gonna happen.

Wow! This machine was getting louder! I definitely needed these earplugs. The noise is getting on my nerves. I'm tired of this. Are we done yet?

Back to thanking God. As people roll through my mind, I just started thanking God for them and praying for them. I drift off into a semi-slumber and once again feel the drool on my lips about to drip down! What?! Oh my goodness. That just cannot happen. We don't want the test to fail because of drool! Get it together girl. I think about people who are paralyzed or can't use their body the way they want; who can't even stop their own drool. I feel terrible for them and commence praying for them. How awful. I'm humbled that God chose my life path for me. But for the grace of God, go I.

Finally! We're finally done. My next appointment is scheduled for Wednesday of this week. I'm told to take my time sitting up. Wait to let the blood flow and make sure I'm not light-headed. Yeah, I'm light-headed all right just to be sitting up again. What a great feeling. The nurse asked if I have any itching or feel like I'm having an allergic reaction to the dye.

*Dye? What dye?* I think to myself. *You never gave it to me. Should I tell her? If I do, I'll have to get back in the big machine.* So I ask instead, "So the dye, did it show anything?" She said they are reading the results and the doctor will let me know.

"Okay," I said while thinking that the dye must have been clear as I never saw it. At least I hope it was clear. I do not want to do this again! Just in case they forgot the dye, I walk swiftly back to the changing closet, hurriedly dressed, and got ought of there! My next appointment was scheduled on Wednesday of that week to speak with the doctor and get the results.

Wednesday is here; a beautiful sunshine-filled day. No one should get disturbing news on a day like this. Heads up, think positive. God's got this all in His hands. Evan and I arrive and I get checked into the crowded waiting room. Finally, my name was called and we went to meet with the doctor and nurse in his office. Turns out I'm not dying of the dreaded disease I googled. The verdict is DCIS, stage 1 cancer. I feel like I've fallen into the dirt. In my mind, I have just fallen down on the side of the road and am sitting in some pretty light-brown dirt. It is stage 1. That's a blessing…right? I try and make myself concentrate on the doctor and listen to what he's saying. Wow. I'm in a state of disbelief. I'm loaded up with information and leave with a new appointment to see the surgeon the following week.

Once we left the office, there was a hall that has a bathroom on it. I told Evan I needed to use the restroom. When in there, I looked at myself in the mirror. I didn't look any different. I'm speechless. I make up in my mind that I'm determined to figure this out… somehow.

At home, I love to sit on the porch, so this is where I find myself after that appointment. I'm googling DCIS and all the other sites for any and all info I can find. After all, I am going to be a well-educated patient on this disease and whatever process I must go through. I found a blog site that's annoyingly cool to read. I'm annoyed that I'm having to find this information. It's cool that other people use this site for people like me. Ugh!

That next day, I was in the house alone and taking a shower. I looked down at my breasts and realized this may be one of the few times I have left to look at them as they were. All of a sudden, I got mad with God and had myself a nice little pity party/temper tantrum. I started stomping my feet and pounding on the wall of the shower with my right and hollering, "God, what are you doing? Why are you doing this? I don't want to do this! I don't have time for this! I don't want this!"

I then looked up and found myself with my left hand raised in praise to God. So then I said to him, "Okay. I will praise you. I'm gonna do this. I love you…but I'm still mad at you, God. I'm mad at you!'

In hindsight, I am most grateful to God for allowing me to have my venting session. I mean it's not like he didn't know it was going to happen. Thank you, Lord.

Mother's day weekend is coming up. I must admit, I'm not in the best of moods right now; being very sarcastic. Well, happy Mother's Day to me…'bout to lose my mother's boobs.

I texted my boss and a coworker to let them know what I'm dealing with. You know, just in case they don't hear from me on Monday…or *all* of next week. You never know, I just may not be able to mentally make it in. Of course, they are sympathetic and want to help. Nothing to be done. Just keep my mind lifted in prayer, I tell them. The mind is a wonderful yet terrifying thing. It can take you to places you never thought you'd go. Into depths of thinking you had no idea even existed in your psyche! Yes, any and all who wanted to know what they could do for me at that time, I told them to pray for my mind.


On Tuesday, May 16, I went back into the office. One of our coworkers approached me and wanted to know if I would talk about my cancer diagnosis at the next company meeting which was coming up on Friday. What? Does he not realize I am still trying to digest this information myself? Does he not realize I am currently "pouting" with God? So I looked at him and politely said, "If God gives me something to say, then I will. Otherwise, this woman has nothing to say." At the time I said this, I felt sure I was *not* going to be hearing anything from God. I was thinking that God and I are not currently speaking to one another. Well…I'm not speaking to him. He is continually blessing me and allowing me to have my temper tantrum. I'm pretty sure he won't give me anything to say to anyone right now. Right? One would think by now, I would know better about how God operates. Was I in for an awakening.

That Thursday afternoon I was sitting at my desk looking out my office window talking to God about a work situation. So yes, at this point I've decided I'll stop pouting. I need him. Hallelujah. Out of "nowhere," he dropped into my spirit what He wants me to say at the meeting tomorrow. Wait a minute, God, we weren't even talking about that subject. So I practiced all evening that night for what I was going to say. Of course, it didn't go as I planned.

First off, I got up so very confidently to speak and my mind went completely blank for a good fifteen or so seconds, I had nothing. God took over and it went as he planned. Strangely enough, I spoke of my temper tantrum in the shower to relate to all listening to how God and my relationships work. It's how I relate to him and how he answers me. Since that time, God has been showing up and showing out in my life! I've been getting texts, emails, phone calls and so many conversations from others about my diagnosis. I take every chance available to tell of his goodness in the midst of the storm that he chose me specifically to walk through. Occasionally, I found myself thinking, *I sure hope God knows what He's doing 'cause I'm not sure about this next step at all!* On the flip side of that is he chose me, so he must know that I can handle it. I'll do my best.

My next appointment is on Thursday, May 25, with the oncologist, Dr. Sam. It was an eye-opener visit for me. First of all, we pulled up to this office and I noticed what the signage outside the building showed. It has the word *cancer* on it. It dawned on me that we're really at a cancer facility. I'm really here. Whoa, getting a little light-headed. This is real stuff. I told Evan that I needed a minute. So we sat there in the car and he waited patiently while I pulled myself mentally together to go in.

Once in, we got checked in, did new patient paperwork, and sat down. I proceeded to read a book that I had previously downloaded on my iPad. After some time, I heard a female checking out. She's laughing and talking with the nurses. I looked up to see who this lively person is. It's a female who lost all her hair. Bald scalp, no eyelashes, no eyebrows, big, beautiful brown eyes, and absolutely gorgeous skin. *Oh boy*, I thought to myself, *that could be me in the next few months.* Yikes! I'm starting to get light-headed again. *Hold on girl,* I told myself. *Look at her. She seems to be healthy. She's laughing and joking with the staff.* This pep talk is not working. My goodness, my heart is racing now. Am I sweating? I think I'm actually having a panic attack! I tell Evan I'm going to the restroom, and I took off to find the nearest one!

In the restroom, I talked to myself, dropping tears, quoting scriptures to myself, and even asking God to hurry and come help me because I'm freaking out! I even gave myself the pep talk: "Who do you think you are to be in here freaking out? There are those who are going through a lot worse than you. Babies and children go through cancer every day. Get over yourself! You told God you would do this, so buck up and do it!" *Lord, help me!*

Eventually, I calmed down, washed my face, and told myself, "You got this. Come on, Jesus. You lead, I'll follow…on shaky legs, but I'm following you." Finally, I got myself somewhat together enough to go back to the waiting room. All the while, I was hoping the young lady is gone. She was. Now you, the reader, don't get this part twisted. The issue was not her. She was doing fine; looking healthy and was laughing. The issue was *me!*

My name is called, and we go in to see the surgeon. It was okay. While waiting for her to come into the room, I was reading some of the material booklets they had on that shelf that sits on the wall. I should not have done that. I read one that was titled *What to Expect When You Have Cancer.* Not a good idea considering the state of mind I was in at that time. I tried to be brave and thumb through it. My knees got weak as if they turned to water and I needed to sit down. I got light-headed again. Oh boy.

At this point, I have gotten extremely annoyed with myself. All of this light-headed crap is getting on my nerves! Needless to say, I put that pamphlet back on the shelf. When Dr. Shortin arrives in the room, she brought with her the patient nurse and one other lady that I don't remember what her part in all of this was. Dr. Shortin proceeds to tell me an abbreviated version of what's going on and what my surgical options are. She then asked if I have an idea of what I wanted to do. I told her what my thoughts were. She seemed a little amazed and laughed while replying well, you sound definite. Yes, it's definite, I replied. She and I then made a game plan from that point forward for my surgery.

Thank you, God, for Evan! When we got home from this visit, I asked Evan what his thoughts were on what I should do. He has this way of looking at me that makes me feel like I can do anything and succeed at it. I know what some people would say to that: "No, he doesn't. He looks mean!" LOL. He looked at me and said, "Whatever you decide to do for you is fine with me. I just want you healthy and well." Boom!

In that particularly vulnerable state of mind I was in, there is no better answer than he could have given me. Evan really has been my stable and comforting helpmate during these many doctor's office visits and consultations. It makes me think about how omniscient God is. He knew all those years ago when Evan and I so naively got married, that He was going to have some serious teachings, healings, growing, and directing to do in our lives. Again, thank you, Lord.

All my life, I have been shockingly terrified of snakes. It takes phobia to another level how afraid I am. When I see one, I freak out, running in the opposite direction with flailing arms and hollering loud enough to make the loudest baby envious of my cries. I get the heebie-jeebies, and my skin crawls. *Ugh!* Whenever I see black cords, wires, argyle socks, or even belts, they are inanimate objects; but in my stressed-out mind, they are moving. I have been known to have nightmares. My children and my husband know this and have unfortunately witnessed this on several accounts.

One Saturday, I was sitting on the porch talking with Brayden and his wife, Trinity. I love sitting outside and I do so quite often. Therefore, I know where every stick, limb, or branch is located in the yard. I even know what tree has roots coming out of the ground. The sticks, limbs, and branches should not be moving unless the wind is blowing them around. The wind was not blowing this Saturday. The day was calm, beautiful, and sunny.

As Brayden is talking, I was looking at the yard. I noticed a limb start to move. I immediately realized the black/white thing was not a limb and it was slithering. "Brayden!" I yelled while grabbing his leg…or maybe it was his arm.

He stops talking, looks at me, and calmly says, "Where's the snake, Mom?" Then he proceeded to look into the yard where my eyes are laser-focused. At this moment, something happened to me that has never happened before. I felt a roaring come up through my feet and into my body and into my spirit. It's like I heard, "*No*, you will not be afraid. You will fight this, and you will win." I immediately realized what I was hearing wasn't about the snake.

At that moment, I made a decision to watch what was happening in the yard. Brayden has now left the porch and returned with a gardening hoe. He then walked towards the snake which, at this time, has gone behind the tree.

I yelled, "Get, it, get it!"

Once the snake saw Brayden, it took off, slithering really fast. Brayden hits it. Then I started yelling, "Cut his head off! Cut it off! Here again, sorry, animal and pest lovers. You don't know my level of fear, so don't judge me too harshly. I then watched as Evan comes to aid in the killing and disposal of the snake in the woods.

This is all amazing to me that I watched it happen! It is even more amazing to me that I can sit here and type this without breaking out in a sweat or having my skin crawl. I have never don't that before. To watch all of that play out, wow. You have no idea how much that moment cost. Thank you, Jesus! To this day, I think Trinity may still have bruises on her arm because while all of that was going on, I'm pretty sure I had grabbed her arm and was squeezing it tightly.

For the rest of their visit, Brayden kept watching me closely and asking if I was all right. He has not seen me do that before. He's not used to this level of calm from me after seeing a snake. I also noticed Evan kept checking on me. They are not alone, as I too am amazed. I was amazed at what God just did. Wow. I don't think Evan even slept that night. When I went to bed, he was sitting on side of the bed looking at me. When I woke the next morning, he was still sitting in that same spot looking at me. LOL. Isn't God awesome?

In June, I met with the reconstructive surgeon, Dr. Gateaux. That was quite the visit! He spoke of the different options available to me. Evan and I watched a movie about what to expect during the process and after the surgeries. Home care, tubes, drains, measuring fluids, and breast expansions. Wow. So glad I did my trusty internet Google homework, so this wasn't quite the shocker. Otherwise, I would have been overwhelmed and devastated!

The funny thing is Evan and I got to hold and feel the saline breasts. If you want to consider this to be funny. I never thought I'd get to actually touch a fake boob let alone consider having them in my body! This is real life here! All in all, this was definitely one of the better visits I've had. Very informative and interesting stuff. Probably more so because his focus was on the "other side of the journey" rather than the uphill side. I like Dr. Gateaux, sounds like he knows his profession. Not to mention he's not bad on the eyes either.

I just got a visual when I typed the words *uphill side.* I see a cancer diagnosis being the uphill side. The actual surgery process is the top of the hill. The downhill side is the recovery. Back down on smooth flatlands moving on with life. Next!

And the appointments continue. Did I mention that during all of this time and appointments, I'm praying for healing from God so I don't need to go through with the surgery? Well, I am praying for just that to happen. I do believe he will heal me. In my years of walking and looking at God, I know that sometimes his healing is not always how we see or think it will be. Perhaps his healing will be in me going through this experience in order to heal another avenue of my life. Perhaps his healing will be in my physical body being touched and the cancer gone. I don't know. What I do know is I am healed. He is my Jehovah-Rophe. Whatever his will is, I am healed. Knowing this, why do I have moments of sadness? Why do I get annoyed when I think about this…which is daily? Why do I feel my body has failed me? The only answer I can come up with is because I am human and my flesh is weak. I wish I were stronger. Some people tell me that I am a strong person. When they say this, I think to myself, If I were not as strong as they say, would God have chosen someone else to walk this storm? Could I have then stayed under his radar and not been chosen for this? Maybe given something a little lighter to bear? I don't know. I am who he made, and he made me this way—strong. Thus, I will carry the banner and do him as proud as I can. Come doubts, tears, fears, praises, joys, happiness, stumbling, healings, and testimonies. To God be the glory!

Kids—they do say the most interesting and thought-provoking things. After telling two of my nieces ages eleven and thirteen about my diagnosis and how I may be coming to stay with them for a while to recuperate, the eleven-year-old Sallie said the funniest thing. Apparently after she thought about it for a moment, she says very dramatically, "Wait! They're going to cut off your breasts! How are you going to woo uncle Evan?" Y'all, this little girl was very serious. Too funny.

Well, it was sooo funny to me but not so funny to my sister, Stacey. She was more interested in how her daughter knew about "wooing" someone and what exactly she meant by that term.

As I was on my way out the door, the thirteen-year-old Leasia then asked a very thought-provoking question, "Are you scared?'

Now, this I find interesting. My answer to her was "No, I have faith in our God." However, as I was driving, I began thinking about her question. All this time, the thought to be afraid had not crossed my mind since I had that panic attack during my first visit to the cancer office. Wow. Every time someone has asked what they can do for me, I always ask them to pray for my mental state of mind. I realized at that moment, prayer works! Thank you to all those that prayed for my mind. I have experienced the following emotions: surprise, annoyance, aggravation, and confusion. I have questioned myself as to if I was doing the right thing and making the right choices. I have fought off moments of depression. I do believe my desire to fight this cancer kicked in after my initial diagnosis and I haven't let myself go back there. I've got to fight to live. I've got to show all who are looking that my Savior really does save. He's saving my spirit, my sanity, my mind, my life, and my everything! I've got no time to devote to fear. He has called me to the plate to play, and I've got to represent Him well. Glory hallelujah!

In June, I am at work, and I get the dreaded phone call. They have scheduled my surgery for Thursday, July 13 at 7:30 a.m. Wow.

I need a moment. I went to the restroom (anyone else here notic-
ing that I have a bathroom theme going…I only realized that in
typing up my journal how I keep typing the word restroom. I guess
that's where God and I have our best conversations). Anyway, I'm
in the restroom talking to Him and quoting scriptures over myself.
I remember saying to God, "Okay, this is it. Am I doing the right
thing? You can show up anytime now and stop this, and I will be fine.
Anytime, God."

I reminded myself of today's motivation that I had just read
about an hour ago. Interestingly enough, the subject was titled "What
Is In, Must Come Out." See how great God is? See how intentional
he is to me? He knew I'd get that call and he set my day up for just
that appointed time with that devotional. My God, He is awesome!
I used that subject line to remind myself of who God is and that he
knows exactly what he is doing. Yep, you guessed it. I started dancing, shouting, and praising God in that restroom. I just couldn't hold
it in. I had praise, and I had to let it out! At one point, I remember
telling myself, "Calm down, girl. You are at work. Be quiet." It did
not work. Sometimes you just gotta let the spirit have its way!

I have one of the sweetest nephews. We call him Li'l C as he
was named after his dad, who is my brother, Big Ceasar. Li'l C and
I were talking. It's Father's day and he basically called me because
he couldn't find his dad. He wanted to know if I knew where he
was. As usual in our conversations, we ended up talking a long while
about some of everything. In the conversation, we were discussing
my cancer diagnosis. His sweet words were so uplifting. He said to
me, "Well, Auntie, you are one of the strongest women I know, and I
also know you've got this. If anybody can do this, you can."

There's that word to describe me again, strong. He didn't know
it, but he helped shore up my foundation and belief that yes, I do
have this. Love that young man! Oh, and Big C is fine. He had just
turned off his phone to get some sleep. He was tired from work.
Praise God.

I received an email from my sister-in-love Jenny. She's married to my brother Idris. In the email, Jenny wrote:

> Hey there, I received your family update on your health. I will surely continue to keep you in my prayers. I admire your strength and faith. You remind me of a quote I read the other day that said a flower has to go through a lot of dirt before becoming a flower. Love you much!

I love this! When I read it, I got the visual of a flower coming up through the dirt into the sunshine. My response to her was this:

> LOL! I love that! I'm learning that in the process of coming through the dirt, there are wonderful blessings to be found. Pushing through the dirt makes one strong and stretches you to grow in faith that when I get through this dirt, the "son" will shine upon me even more! Love ya!

God favors me. For a couple of weeks now, I've been looking for a particular style of shoe. I've gone to several locations but just couldn't find the "right one." They are either too loose, too tight, too short, not the right color, heel height, or something. After meeting my sister Stacey at Dexter's house, Stacey gives me this package from our oldest sister, Tatiana (aka Tati, for short). I opened the package and guess what was in it? Yes! The exact shoes I had been looking for. I tried them on right then and there in the parking lot, and they fit perfectly. Thank you, Tati, and thank you, God. Favor ain't fair, but it sure feels good on me!

It was Sunday, and I awoke with a pounding headache. After lying in bed trying to see if perhaps this would go away on its own, I finally give up. Or in all honesty, I gave up and got up because I had to use the restroom. Oh my goodness, the shoulder and backache! Where did this come from? Now, I'm walking like I'm one hundred years old, all bent over and moaning. I don't understand. Did

I perhaps get in a fight last night and don't remember? Did I have a nightmare and fought some forgotten foe?

I looked at Evan, and he seemed fine, so I guess I didn't fight him. Whoa. Now I have aches everywhere from across my shoulders up. The phone is ringing…oh my aching head. Stop! I realized I have some peppermint oil that one of my coworkers said is good for headaches. Yes! I also remember that I have some muscle rub I got from my brother Vario. Double yes! Off to the hot shower I go. Afterward, I applied peppermint oil to my temples and muscle rub to my shoulders and neck.

Now, pressing onward to church. I may be smelling like mint and menthol, but I'm going to get my praise in! Service was awesome, and God was moving all in the building this Sunday. Great singing, awesome teaching, wonderful worship, and inspiring prayers. Afterward, one of the church mothers asked if she could pray over me. Absolutely! She did so by praying a beautiful healing prayer over me. Once done, she said she was looking forward to my testimony. I told her I couldn't wait to tell it to her! Yes, Lord! I was just full of *him*. The devil really tried to stop me from this beautiful service, but not today, Satan!

# CHAPTER 7

# I Will Praise the Lord at All Times!

One night after I got home from work, I was sitting there, doubting myself and asking God if I was hearing Him correctly. I'm supposed to have this surgery and get this cancer cut out of me. I didn't want to make a misstep in this process and I just needed him to speak to me one more time.

After a while, I started scrolling through Facebook. I saw where someone had posted a video from their pastor's sermon. I decided to check it out. *O Lord, how excellent is thy name!*

In the video, the first thing he said was "This won't hit everybody. Someone needs to hear this and this is for them." He proceeds to ask, "Are you in a season where God is taking away something?" He went on to say that whenever God wants to bring abundance, he *cuts*. Whenever he prunes a thing and moves it out from your life, it's because there is a tremendous fruitfulness that he's wanting to bring into your life (John 15). He said, "God will bring you more by removing what's there. God is always going to take you bigger, better, and greater." *Wow!* I got my answer from God. Thank you, Lord, for you are greatly to be praised. Hallelujah!

July 13, 2017, at 4:00 a.m., was the day. This was the morning of the surgery. I awoke and used the little packets they give you to wash your skin with before you're having surgery. I feel sad but am doing my best to handle it and not show it. I'm thinking this is the last time I will see the breasts that God gave me. I am still depending on God to show up and stop this. If he doesn't, then I trust he has the plan. He knows what he is doing. I also make sure I have my gospel music CDs that I have instructed Stacey and Evan to play when I get to my hospital room. I want nothing but praise and worship music playing in my room. I am healed and thus I will praise and worship the Lord. That means the atmosphere must be set for him!

Once Evan and I arrived at the hospital, I felt at peace. I was not afraid. I actually found myself thinking excitedly about what God is going to do. How will He show up in me through this? I am about to be healed but I don't know the details of how He will do it. I can't help this excitement…is this even normal?

I get checked in and proceed to get dressed for surgery. I'm lying in the bed and watching the hospital staff do all the things they do. Getting me hooked up; blood pressure; IV drip taped to my arm; etc. Our pastor, John Smith (yes, that's his real name), and his wife, Jeannie came in to chat with me and prayed over me. It touched my heart that they would take the time to come pray me off to surgery so early in the morning. Also in the room, is my girlfriend of over thirty years, Keishan. She is always good for my soul as she can make you laugh at just about anything. Talk about a prayer warrior! When Keishan prays, the angels take it straight to Jesus. She is not playing! As I'm led away for surgery, there stands all of them with Evan and Stacie. Thank you, God, for family and friends in a time like this. I have no doubt I am covered in prayer.

I awoke some six hours later in my hospital room, and it was done. God did not show up and stop the surgery. Not sure how I feel about this. Nonetheless, he was there in the surgery, and I am healed. I'm lying there drugged up, but I hear my worship CD playing in the background. Keishan had gone out and bought a plaque for me and on it were the words "You Are Healed." Yes, thank you, Lord!

The following morning, one of the nurses tells me that I was quite the entertainer while coming off the anesthesia meds they had me on. Talking out of my head and making my family laugh. She also told me she enjoyed the music and there was church worship going on in my room last night. This makes me feel great!

Before we leave the hospital, the physical therapist team came in to show me how to do exercises to prevent lymphedema. *Ugh!* I don't like this. I remember talking to God in my mind that He had better know what he was doing. Of course he does, but I feel a tiny bit better feeling like I'm telling the Almighty what to do.

Evan and I are now settled in at Stacey's house. I have four drains coming out of my body! I feel like an alien. Mentally and physically. It is quite interesting, though. Who knew the medical field had these kinds of contraptions and things going on? Drains have to be squeezed twice a day into measuring cups. Then that information is to be recorded in the medical journal they give you. To move about, I had to have a specially made top that was provided to me by the hospital. Wonder of wonders, this top has four pockets on it. One for each of the drains to sit in so they don't get caught on anything. Not that I'm doing too much moving, but they do make maneuvering about easier.

Sitting here in bed, a week after surgery. Today was a rough day. Evan and Stacey have been pretty much taking care of me along with Leasia and Sallie. I have quit taking the pain pills as I do not like that feeling of being high. If I'm going to be high, it's going to be high in the spirit; not high on some man-made medication. (Should have told myself that more than thirty years ago…LOL!) I'm not eating much as everything I've tried tastes like either a mouth full of cotton or bits of straw…*no* taste at all!

After several failed attempts to eat, it appears that Activia peach yogurt is great! I can taste it. A couple of family members have suggested turnip greens and the pot juices from it. I haven't tried it yet.

Savannah, my niece from Georgia, is Jenny and Idris's daughter. She came to town this weekend to give Leasia and Sallie some help.

One day, they were "assisting" me as I was doing my at-home exercise therapy. One of the exercises includes lifting both arms forward and up as high as I can and holding them in that position for a few seconds. On this particular day, my three nieces were doing them with me, and we were counting as we went. I had lifted my arms forward to a little less than shoulder height. I was gritting my teeth to hold that pose for a few seconds. I happened to look up at my nieces and noticed they were gritting their teeth and concentrating on their arms as if they were in pain too! I immediately lost it. My arms fell down, and I dissolved in laughter…so funny! I love these young ladies. You have no idea. Thank you, God. Bless them, Lord.

Earlier today, Evan and I went to the house to check on things. All is well. However, I did find myself in the bathroom crying. Yes, I'm in the restroom…again. I had gone in there to get something only to realize that the last time I was in there, I had two God-given breasts that were now gone. Oh, the tears! I choose to trust God through this experience. Yes, the tears are falling, but in him I trust.

Revelation moment: I think I just figured out why I seem to use bathrooms for more than just the obvious reason. I go in there to bathe myself in God's love. Aah! All my life, I've used bathrooms as a place for temper tantrums, praise time, prayers, quiet time, answers, and consultations from the Maker. I find this revelation very interesting.

It's now a little over two weeks since the surgery. Big C brings over some homemade chicken and rice. It is delicious…I can *taste* it a little bit, especially the pepper. Hey, pepper is a taste, and this dish is tasting like manna from heaven right now! I kept saying "Thank you, God" while eating it. Big C said our mama, who's been deceased for over twenty years, told him to cook it for me. He may have been joking, but I believe it. It was just that good!

I'm doing good. Exercising as instructed for my shoulder, arm, and chest muscles. Evan and I are now back at home. I'm not in the best of shape, but I am better. I can do this. After all, God got me into this, and He will continue to see me through it. He already told me so.

My taste buds have gone on hiatus. Since that chicken and rice from Big C, nothing tastes good. I am surviving off of Activia yogurt and ginger ale. I have lost weight; although I'm pretty sure my doctors would not think this is good.

Well, hallelujah! Evan cooked some homemade fried chicken, and Aunt Faith had sent some turnip greens to go with the chicken. Oh my goodness it was good. I could taste all of it. Thank you, God. Chocolate is a no-no item. It tastes horrible to me. Remember the straw taste I described earlier? Well, that's exactly what chocolate tastes like…ick! I guess that isn't a bad thing though.

It's now August and Evan and I are back in the plastic surgeon's office of Dr. Gateaux. He wants me to go back to surgery. Oh no! He says he will need to reopen one of my wounds, clean out the dead tissue, then refill it back and stitch it all closed again. I *really* do *not* want to do this. I am getting frustrated and seriously trying to close the lid on the chapter!

The surgery is to be scheduled for later this week whenever he can get an operating room. His office will call to let me know.

We leave his office and Evan dropped me off at the hair salon. I have not been released for driving so he is still driving me around. This hair salon I was going to is a great place to get your hair done without all of the noise and drama you sometimes encounter. It's owned by an anointed Christian woman by the name of Devine Brandon. You can see God's presence all in her and on her. Today, while riding to the salon, I was thinking about God and what is it he's wanting me to do or know during this season. My mind was just all over the place thinking. My thoughts were that I wished he would put a rush on things so I can get over this journey and on to something else. Is there something that I'm supposed to be doing that I'm not learning or understanding? Why are we still doing this season?

Eventually, I arrive at the salon. I go in as usual, speak to everyone, and sit down to await my beautician. The owner and another lady were talking about God (which is not unusual in this salon). I pulled out my iPad and proceeded to start reading one of the books I have downloaded. My beautician arrives. She gets my hair done pretty quick and I'm on my way out the door. As I get to the door, the owner stops me. She asked if she can talk to me. I said "Of course" and followed her outside the salon. She told me that when God gives her something, she is obedient to it. She then gave me two scriptures: Jeremiah 2 and Psalm 23. She said to read them in the Amplified Bible and that God wants me to know not to look at the natural. God doesn't want me to look at the natural of what he's taken away because he is going to replace all of it. He has so much more that he's going to do for me and give me.

Oddly enough (or maybe not so odd), she said I should keep a journal of this time. I find this interesting since journaling this time has been exactly what I have been doing. I had even been toying with the idea to stop journaling and now this. Wow. I will keep posting my days' events. She goes on to say that I should read Psalm 23 and stay there, dwell in that scripture, and soak it up. She then said something that intrigued me, "You can't heal others if you haven't healed yourself." I'm not sure where this statement is coming from or going, but I'm willing and open to receiving whatever God is doing.

Lastly, she told me that she keeps hearing the word *books* about me, books with an *s*. *Whoa!* This could be so many things to me. I am definitely waiting on God to see where he is going with that. She then asks if she can anoint my head with oil. I said yes. Wow. I now know this is God! I say this because no one knows of my personal, secret desire to be anointed before I go into this second surgery! God is awesome! He knows my heart and I am so humbled. Thank you, God. Thank you, Mrs. DB, for being obedient to the moving of the Spirit. May God continue to bless you and your business ventures!


Today started off rough with the visit to Dr. Gateaux. Now I'm sitting here smiling and typing. Glory to God! I also have the Amplified Bible pulled up and am reading the Word from the Lord. He is doing mighty things and I am in the mix...little ole me is in God's plan. Hallelujah!

The call came today for my second surgery. I am to be there at 1:00 p.m. tomorrow. It's all good because after yesterday's praise at the salon, I am at peace. Thank you, Jesus...let's do this so you can get all the glory!

We are all here for my surgery, waiting. I am blessed. Today, I have a new crew of prayer warriors: Evan; Stacey; Aunt Faith; Dexter's wife, Shelley; our two grandsons; and my brother-in-law, Lee, and his wife, Rose.

My surgery went great. Feeling woozy-headed but good.

On the way home, Evan, Aunt Faith, and I stopped at a local restaurant called Coach's Place and ordered food to go. I do remember tasting that plate of food and it was delicious. Thank you, God!

Since I've been home, I've been studying Psalm 23 and quoting it to myself. I've gotten more out of it each time. There's a part that says, "Yea though I walk through the valley of the shadow of death, I will fear no evil…" Upon thinking about this, it brought to mind a sermon I once heard during the same week of my original cancer diagnosis. The speaker said, "God says to go through this storm in the valley but not to dwell there." Well, thank you, Lord. This is so encouraging to me. Tonight, I was studying Jeremiah 29:11, which says, "For I know the plans I have for you, says the Lord; plans for peace and wellbeing and not for disaster; to give you a future and a hope." Praise the Lord!

Monday, August 21, is eclipse day. *This is the day the Lord has made. I will rejoice and be glad in it!* God is amazing. Evan and I are outside, sitting on the porch, awaiting this blessed, historical event. This is a once-in-a-lifetime event, and of course it was all over the media. It was amazing. Once it was really, really dark, the crickets even stopped chirping and you could see the birds flying back to their nests. All was calm. Then, it got really quiet for about thirty seconds. Then, the moon moved on and the sun came back out. Amazing! My God, you do some wonderful work!

Evan went back to work this week. After almost two months of being out to help take care of me. When I tell you this man took his vows of "in sickness and in health" seriously, believe it. I constantly thank God for Evan.

This week also marks my last week at home. Yes! I plan to return to work next week. A lot of my family keeps asking me if I am ready or commenting I should take more time. No, I don't think so. I'm ready to get back into the work grind. Slow and steady.

# CHAPTER 8

# I Stay Amazed at God

I'm sitting here tonight, studying and absorbing Psalm 23. The version that I'm studying has study notes at the end of the Psalm. One of the notes is "In ancient times, it was customary for the host to provide his guests with olive oil to put on their heads. The Lord blesses and anoints his believers with the Holy Spirit, whom oil symbolizes, to prepare them for his services." Wow! When I read this, it was like a lightning spark when through me. Thank you, Jesus. I thought back to when the owner of the salon had anointed my head with oil. *Whoop!* Does this mean God is going to use me? I hope so! Of course in my mind, I want to be like Devine, the salon owner. God will give me something to tell someone; and they, too, will be happy I told them. Hmmm. I am pretty sure it won't be like that at all. Knowing God, he's got something different planned, and I'm most likely way off base. I do find it interesting that I was listening to a television evangelist, and he was talking about levels. How God can take you to different levels in your life. Maybe God is about to take me to another level for his good.

In Psalms 23 (Amplified Bible), the words "he refreshes and restores my life" stand out to me. My spirit jumped when I read that part—*restores*. Goodness, I just realized that God is restoring me! All that I think I have lost, he is restoring back. Yes, I know I've heard this many times in this season, yet tonight, it really is cemented in my mind more so than ever! Hallelujah! Thank you, God. I can't wait to see what he is doing next!

September comes in, and I'm sitting here tonight listening to a sermon titled "It's Not What It Looks Like." It was powerful and an on-time message for me. I feel like God is talking to me and he is answering some questions I've had in my mind as well as thoughts that have been battling in my head, one being that in today's mail, there was one of those "phishing" checks. You know, the kind where they send you a check but it's actually a loan. If you cash it, then you now owe that company a certain amount of money to be paid back over a certain period of time. This check was for a substantial amount of money. I normally tear these up and throw these in the trash. That day, I didn't do that. So the sermon I was listening to was right on time! He was talking about being tempted yet not giving in. Things are not always quick and easy; they are not what they look like. You have to know the story and read the fine print. Wow. Thank you, God, for answering the battle in my mind. You know I tore up that check, and in the trash those bits and pieces went.

In this sermon, the speaker went on to talk about Jesus and the woman at the well and how Jesus went out of his way to go through Syria to that particular well. Even though Jesus was a Jew, and at that time, the Syrians and the Jews didn't have anything to do with one another. Jesus went to that well to wait on her. The speaker made it a point to say that this is how Jesus is with us. He waits on us. Even when we are in our devilish ways; doing what we went, even the wrong things. Jesus waited. I'm so glad he waited on me!

God is amazing. The following is my timeline for the last of the month of September. I'm still amazed today at how God does what he does for just little me:

September 17: Sunday services, and the subject of the sermon is "I Believe." It was moving and powerful. My personal belief right now is that God is healing my family. He has healed me. I believe the recent attacks on our families are over. I believe I will continue to stand in the gap and fight for my family. Amen.

September 20: The blessing is in the breaking. That's what I'm watching tonight. The teacher said, "Anyone who is in their breaking season, God is going to bless you. He doesn't take you through the breaking unless He's about to bless you. El Shaddai. God who is more than enough. He is a God of overflow. David said my cup runneth over. You can be following divine instructions right into the store. If you're going through a storm on divine instructions, you are in the blessings. This storm is not to destroy you. It is to show you him on another dimensional level. Believe it." Wow!

September 21: Today's daily devotional was titled "Believe." *What?* It's like this was written expressly for me. In it were these words. Someone has just come out of a storm and God is about to turn everything about you for the good. Someone watching this has been saying the word believe and now it's time.

September 22: Not only do I hear the word believe, but I also keep seeing the word believe! It was even in Walmart on a card which I just happened to glance at as I was strolling through the card section trying to get to the other side of the store. I also heard it in the lyrics of a song while listening to the radio. I was reading a simple story and there the word again was—*believe.*

Now at this point, let me tell you, readers. I know all of these instances taken alone are not that impressive. However, when you put them in the timeline of how often they were happening with me in those few days, and the fact I didn't tell you all of them, trust me. This time frame was mind-blowing! Hallelujah!

It is so mind-blowing that a song came to mind that week that I started playing it over and over again. I just couldn't get enough of it. Some of the words are as follows:

> Oh, you amaze lord you amaze
> With your presence with your power
> You never fail you never cease
> So amaze me I believe in you
> Forever you will stand
> Your kingdom has no end
> O holy God, I stay amazed

You are so much more than words could ever say
O holy God, I pour out my praise
On the one who never ceases to amaze
I'm pouring out my praise on you
I'm pouring out my love on you
I'm pouring out my praise on you
I'm pouring out my love on you

It's now the month of October and today's daily devotion is to expect Christmas this month. It says God is gifting His people so be ready. Okay.

I didn't think too much about this until I got to work one morning. One of my coworkers had decided to "gift" me with a CD that she had heard and thought I'd like. *Wow.*

Then another friend "gifted" me with a purple (my favorite color) carry bag that she saw while out shopping and thought of me. *What!*

Our grandson, who was five years old at the time, gifted me with the best gift. He wrote with his crayon on a piece of typing paper the words "Grandma, you are LOVE," then gave it to me. He actually used the words that this picture is a "gift for you, Grandma." This is awesome! No, my *God* is awesome!

As stated above, I've been listening to the song "I Stay Amazed." One night, I was watching TBN's Dove Awards. The group that sings "I Stay Amazed" was on there. But tonight, they were singing, "Jesus, What a Beautiful Name It Is," another beautiful song. So all this week, I've been singing both songs pretty much every night, replaying them several times on YouTube. Thank you, Lord, for the gift of these songs. Christmas!

On Thursday of this same week, a very dear family member called me and said she had something for me. Well, I went to her house thinking it was probably a "Thinking of You" card or maybe a book or some small token of love. However, I was wrong! This woman of God hands me a big pink bag full of goodies: a scarf, a coffee mug, an insulated cup, a brooch, a bracelet, a diary or writing journal (yes, I used it [LOL]), a banner, some kitchen goodies, and so much more. Oh my, what a blessing. Yes, it is Christmas for me! Thank you, God, for Mrs. FB. I pray He continually blesses your life and family. You have no idea.

At this point in my diary, I'm hoping you, readers, will understand how God favors me. I sincerely hope you have or will have a relationship with him in this same favor. You have no idea how much I pray this for all of you.

The mind is a wonderful thing, but sometimes we must fight it. What is going on in my mind? There is a serious battle. Depression is not a joke and I pray for anyone who has to deal with it. It comes when it wants to and has no respect for place, people, or time. You have no idea how much I pray about this particular disease. Oh my goodness, help us, Lord!

Today, I was at home doing laundry. I got frustrated and decided to take the larger comforters and spreads to the laundromat, throw them all in the big washer there and get them washed and over with. While there, waiting for them to wash, I noticed a woman across on the other side of the laundromat. I started hating her immediately. Why? She was blessed with these overly large appendages that were sagging in her very nice outfit. I mean *pfft* (I'm sucking my teeth at her), who gets that dressed up to come wash clothes? Her sagging breasts need a bra. Ha! I catch myself judging. Why am I thinking this? I have both complimented and downgraded her in the same breath. I didn't know this woman. I know nothing about her. It's just me in my pissy, depressive, woe-is-me mood, trying to feel sorry for myself. I realize that throughout this day, I had been thinking constantly about things that were depressive and out of my control. This is concerning to me as this is not my normal state of mind. I need help Lord 'cause I can't shake it! At one point, this woman and I caught eyes with one another, and I made myself smile at her. She smiled back. Well, crapdabbit, wouldn't you know it, she's even lovelier when she smiles. *Ugh!*

Earlier this year, the employees of our office were asked to write their stories of how they came to be an employee of the company.

Once all the stories were turned in, they were then created into a book as a Christmas gift for the owners to read at their leisure. I wrote my story; turned it in, and went on about my merry employee way. Later, after it was published, one of the women who read it said my story made her cry tears of happiness. Thank you, Lord, for the way you move. Another person told me it made her laugh and cry all at the same time. Wow. God is amazingly still touching people after all those years ago that I based the story on. She also said something that I find very interesting. She told me that if I ever write anything about anything, she wants to know so she can buy it...*what?* Wait; hold on...what is God doing? I'm getting excited. Thank you, Lord, for your grace and mercy. You truly are amazing!

God is interesting. At one point, I decided I was inserting my own will and desires into this idea. That my writing bits of my life story was not what God wanted me to do. Oh, how devilish our thoughts can be to try and lead us astray.

I was at a birthday breakfast for me thrown by my family. My second oldest sister, Leomie, gifted me with a purple diary. When I saw it, something came over me. Then when I held the diary in my hand, I felt I knew exactly what God was telling me to do with it. I hear ya, Lord. I had no idea how much that purple diary would become a big part of leading to this journey. I love it when God uses others to speak to me.

# CHAPTER 9

# DREAM BOARDS, It's a Live Thing

In January 2019, I attended a vision board event. The title of this event was Dream Board Experience. My cousin is the founder and CEO of a Christian-based business. This vision board event was sponsored by her business. In this gathering of phenomenal women, some were giving their testimonies of how God had changed their lives and how the vision boards were used to "kick off" the blessings God had for them. When deciding to attend this event, I was dubbing myself "doubting Aretha," as I was unsure about going and even more unsure about what to expect. In the end, I decided to go and support my cousin, but I wasn't expecting anything to come out of it. Here again, you would think that at this point and experiences I've had with God in my life, I would know him better than that. Seriously, why did I think I could throw down a gauntlet of saying "I won't be expecting anything to come out" of an event he has sanctioned? When I tell you that God showed up and revealed himself in that room, you have no idea. I just can't even begin to tell you the blessings I received in those two hours of being in that room.

There were some very inspirational and motivational speakers. My God showed himself to be a savior of those who overcame suicide attempts, depression, poverty, and abuse; gained confidence; started their own businesses; and so much more! We did everything from laughing to crying to eating to shouting, and it was all cathartic.

At one point, I was in a line signing up for an upcoming event and found myself shouting praises to God with two other women. I didn't even know them, but the spirit was moving in our conversation and the fellowship was awesome!

For our vision boards, we were to think prayerfully about what we wanted God to do in our lives in the new year. The directive was to think real and think big, not something you can accomplish on your own but something only God can do. One of the inspirational speakers told her story of how she had attended a previous vision board party and had put on her board to travel. At the time, she had no money nor any idea of how she was going to do it. She prayed about it and left it in God's hands. Well, he showed up in her finances by having a ram in the bush for her. She's now an international traveler going all over the world. I follow her on Facebook, and it's awesome to see the world through her lens.

Praying you to continue to have happy and safe trails, my traveling diva friend!

On my vision board, I had previous thoughts of what I wanted to put on mine and how it would look. I was able to find all my pictures, but along the way, the word *family* dropped into my spirit. I ignored it. However, the word family kept repeating itself in my head. Do you know it was about two minutes later that I saw in a magazine the word *family* in large red letters! I immediately cut it out and glued it to my vision board. Then a little while later, I saw a phrase that I cut out and pasted as well. It reads, "Family and Friends, Finding Faith." Wow! Something came over me and I knew. I just had that feeling you get when God is talking to you! This changed the "tone" of my vision board. I knew what I had to do on my fast for 2019! I was going to war for my family in 2019. I felt the calling. God is amazing!

One of the pictures I had cut out for my vision board was a stack of books. I thought I was cutting that picture out because I love to read. I mean I *really* love to read! I remember thinking that this stack of books has titles of some really great literature. As I glue the picture down, I am thinking that I will make it a point to read more non-fiction this year. Jokingly I think to myself that maybe I'll even write a book and then I laughed out loud at my own little private joke. My friend across the table from me asked what I was laughing at. I replied, "Nothing girl. I'm over here making up fantasies." I had no idea that I would be sitting here starting my story the very next month! Of course, at this point, I don't know what I'm going to do with this diary book thing. If nothing else, it will make a good memory for me. Maybe I will have it published for my kids and grands. I have heard that you can do that. We'll see.

Okay, readers, thanks for bearing with me thus far. My last testimony and praise in this diary for you:

While driving home later that month, I was thinking about this book and asking God if this was really what he wanted me to do. I specifically said, "God, if this is what you want, then I will do it. I just need you to tell me and give me a clear sign that I am doing the right thing." It wasn't a minute later, seriously, that an advertisement came on the radio for Christian Faith Publishing. The first lines of the ad said, "Do you have a book to write, a story you've been working on?" *What?* I knew then I had gotten my answer. I continued driving while shouting out in the car, "Thank you, Lord!"

So I got all my diaries together and went through them to pull out the parts of my life I wanted to share. Thus, the story you have just read was created. Is this the end…I have no idea. This was all God's vision, and I'm just following in his guidance.

Speaking of vision, I know it was some serious praying over that vision board meeting before it even started. I say that because I am seeing my vision board come to life in so many areas. If you ever get the chance to attend one, I urge you to pray about it and if so led, do attend. You have no idea.

If you are still reading this, thank you. I wish you a healthy life. Most of all, I pray you too will one day have a diary of praise to tell about your life as well. You have no idea.

# SERVICES that BLESSED ME!

*Each of you should use whatever gift you have received to serve others, as faithful stewards of God's grace in it's various forms. 1 Peter 4:10 NIV*

Billie Jean Styles
billiejean@billiejeanstyles
Billiejeanstyles.com
Billie Jean Bolden, Owner

Genuinely Zoe—864-346-4955
Genuinelyzoe@gmail.com
Genuinelyzoe.org
Alfreda Coleman, CEO/Founder

**United Way Community Resources Hotline—211**
https://211.org

**Prisma Health Cancer Institute—833-379-1483**
Prismahealth.org

**National Red Cross—1-800-RED-CROSS**
www.redcross.org

**Salvation Army—1-800-728-7825**
www.salvationarmy.org

**National Suicide Hotline—1-800-273-TALK**
www.suicidepreventionlifeline.org

# ABOUT THE AUTHOR

Aretha Johnson was born and raised in the part of the United States known as the "Bible Belt of the South." She's a wife of one, mother of two, and counselor and mentor of many. She has been journaling her life as far back as getting her first diary around the age of ten. When she's not somewhere reading, she can usually be found dreaming and planning her next adventure to travel. Whether reading or traveling, she's sure to be munching on Lay's plain potato chips or any variety of fruits. She believes God is her King—her everything.